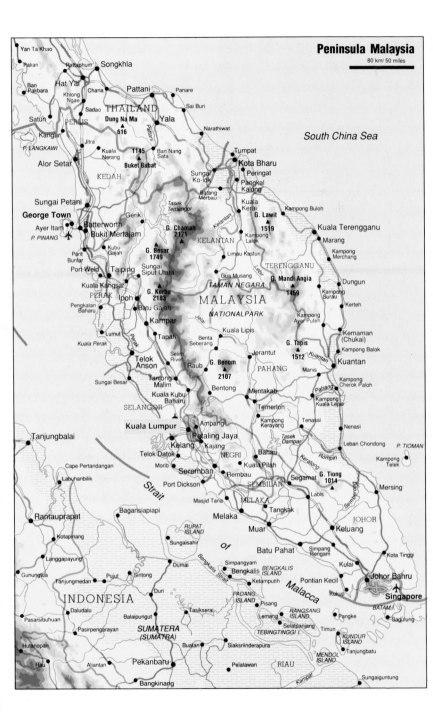

Peninsula Malaysia

80 km/ 50 miles

Yan Ta Khao
Palian
Rattaphum   Songkhla
Ban Pakbara
Hat Yai
Khlong Ngae   Chana   Pattani   Panare
Sadao
Satun   THAILAND   Yala   Sai Buri
PERLIS   Dung Na Ma
616
Narathiwat
Kangar   Jitra   Kuala Nerang   1145   Ban Nang Sata
Alor Setar   Buket Bubat   Sungai Ko-lok   Tumpat
KEDAH   Batang Merbau   Kota Bharu
Peringat
Sungai Petani   Gerik   Kuala Kerai   Pangkal Kalong
George Town   Tasek Temengor   G. Lawit   Kampong Buloh
Ayer Itam   Butterworth   1519   Kuala Terengganu
P. PINANG   Bukit Mertajam   G. Chamah   Kampong Lalok   Marang
Parit Buntar   Kubu Gajah   2171   KELANTAN   Kampong Merchang
Port Weld   G. Besar   Limau Kasturi   TERENGGANU
Taiping   1749   Gua Musang   G. Mandi Angia   Dungun
Kuala Kangsar   Sungai Siput Utara   TAMAN NEGARA   1459   Kampong Surau
PERAK   G. Korbu   MALAYSIA   Kerteh
Pengkalan Baharu   Ipoh   2183   NATIONALPARK   Kampong Ayer Puteh
Batu Gajah   Jelai   Kemaman (Chukai)
Lumut   Kampar   Kuala Lipis   G. Tapis   Kampong Balok
Kuala Perak   Tapah   Benta Seberang   1512   Kuantan
Perak   Selim River   Jerantut   Kampong Cherok Paloh
Telok Anson   G. Benom   Raub   PAHANG   Manis
Sungai Besar   Tanjong Malim   2107   Pahang   Kampong Kuala Lepar
Kuala Kubu Baharu   Bentong   Mentakab   Kampong Kerayong   Nenasi
SELANGOR   Ampang   Temerloh   Tenassi   Leban Chondong   P. TIOMAN
Tanjungbalai   Kuala Lumpur   Petaling Jaya   Tasek Dampar   Kampong Telek
Kelang   Kajang   Bahau   Rompin
Cape Pertandangan   Telok Datok   NEGRI   Kuala Pilah   Keratong   Kampong Telek
Labuhanbilik   Morib   Seremban   Rembau   SEMBILAN   Segamat   G. Tiong   Mersing
Rantauprapat   Port Dickson   1014
Bagansiapiapi   Masjid Tana   MELAKA   Tangkak   Labis   Semberong
Kotapinang   RUPAT ISLAND   Melaka   JOHOR   Keluang
Langgapayung   Sungaisahir   Muar   Simpang Rengam   Kota Tinggi
Gunungtua   Tanjungmedan   Pujut   Sintong   Dumai   Simpangyam   Batu Pahat   Kulai
Duri   Bengkalis   BENGKALIS ISLAND   Pontian Kecil   Johor Bahru
Daludalu   Ketamputih   PADANG ISLAND   Kukup   Singapore
Pasarsibuhuan   Balaipungut   Tasikserai   Pisang   BATAM I.
Hutanopan   Pasirpengarayan   Buatan   RANGSANG ISLAND   Pangke   Sagulung
Riau   Aliantan   Pekanbaru   Siaksriinderapura   Lemang   Selatpanjang   Timun   KUNDUR ISLAND   Tanjungbatu
SUMATERA (SUMATRA)   TEBINGTINGGI I.
Bangkinang   Pelalawan   RIAU   MENDOL ISLAND
INDONESIA   Sungaiguntung

South China Sea

Strait   of   Malacca

Selamat Datang!

Beyond the skyscrapers and ritzy shopping malls, Kuala Lumpur has another face – the quaint and quiet, the rustic and natural. The lesser known appeals can easily escape the eyes of most visitors using the capital city as a transit stop. And unless a Kuala Lumpurian points these attractions out, they often go amiss.

In *Insight Pocket Guide: Kuala Lumpur*, very little goes amiss. For this compact handbook of tailor-made itineraries is designed for the traveller who seeks to see beyond the superficial and explore, in depth, Kuala Lumpur's heart.

As your personal guide, the author, free-lance journalist Shoba Devan, has spent much time exploring the little alley-ways and city outskirts, the mayhem of Chinatown, the sprawling mass of shopping malls and the ethnic corners, to open up to you K.L.'s variety.

In *Insight Pocket Guide: Kuala Lumpur*, Shoba Devan shares with you just how to extract the most out of a few days here. She first acquaints you with the city's initial development from an obscure riverine village to the bustling capital of Malaysia, its people, their religions, lifestyles and culture.

The author then introduces three full-day itineraries which help you get your bearings right around the city. From prominent city landmarks through colourful, noisy Chinatown and to the restive Lake Gardens, these itineraries lead you to K.L.'s oldest mosque, resplendent colonial architecture, the city's best chicken rice and night markets to watch the incredible feats of medicine men.

Then, pick from morning and afternoon tours, which you can combine as you please, to places of interest such as Batu Caves, Little India or Shah Alam. Select from the list of day trips and nightlife recommendations, and you will find your stay in K.L. every bit as wonderful as it is fun. Whether you want to shop till you drop, or trek through tropical forests, Shoba Devan imparts valuable information, offering an insight of behind-the-scenes happenings.

In other sections, you find out the best eateries, the best way to move around the city, etiquette to observe and a glossary of *Bahasa Malaysia* words to help you get around.

This book is meant to tickle your curiosity, so that you will unleash the explorer in you and discover what really makes Kuala Lumpur tick.

Selamat Datang! Welcome!

3

Insight Pocket Guide:

KUALA LUMPUR

First Edition

© 1991 APA Publications (HK) Ltd.

All Rights Reserved

Printed in Singapore by

Höfer Press (Pte) Ltd

Fax: 65-861 6438

INSIGHT *pocket* GUIDES

KUALA LUMPUR

Written by	**Shoba Devan**
Directed by	**Hans Höfer**
Design Concept by	**V. Barl**
Art Direction by	**Karen Hoisington**
Photography by	**Ingo Jezierski**
Editorial Director	**Michael Stachels**

INSIGHT
pocket
GUIDES

Contents

Dear Reader,

Kuala Lumpur is no Athens or Rome. Less than 100 years ago, it was an unrecognisable shanty-town sitting precariously on the edge of a marshy riverbank. But for some unfathomable reason, the people came – Malay farmers, Chinese merchants, British tin miners, Indian railroad workers – making it a cultural polyglot with few parallels. One hundred years later, the migration still has not stopped.

The madness of the traffic and the cosmopolitan crowds pounding the pavements of the city's streets may disguise its origins but Kuala Lumpur's true colours come through during major festivals. Then, far more pervasive loyalties dominate, and the migrants flee to their hometowns or villages to be with their families and loved ones. Kuala Lumpur, or K.L. for short, is reduced to a ghost town; the traffic din dies down and the sidewalks echo a strange silence.

Like other migrants, I moved to K.L. 12 years ago out of sheer necessity. After a childhood in a rural town ensconced in rambling reaches of forest, rubber and oil palm, and then three languid years enjoying Penang island's quaint charm and laid-back living, K.L. was a reluctant choice.

The city it seemed, had nothing going for it; no beaches or countryside; no secrets....and most of all, it did not feel like home. I would make a beeline for the south or the north every chance I got. Like the others, I did not stop to look.

But as I became familiar with the city's smells, sounds and sights, I learnt to look beyond the concrete skyscrapers and saw a rusticity about K.L. Like the small town folk who are drawn to the city, it has retained a certain idyllic charm.

Part of the reason is that among Southeast Asian capital cities, Kuala Lumpur is the smallest and incidentally, the newest. Like some precocious child, it is trying to grow out its shanty-town infancy, yet is unable to shake off the small-town homeliness and hospitality, the most transient phase in urban evolution. That spirit man-

ifests itself subtly – the smile of recognition on the neighbourhood soya bean milk hawker; the spirited political discussions of the local barber; the hammy performances by sidewalk medicine vendors – these, and more, make up a face that is often inscrutable, yet, with time, endearing.

I no longer run away from the city so often these days, even when tradition beckons. I suppose I am no longer the emigrant I once was. K.L. is as home to me now as the forests, estates and beaches used to be. I hope this book will help you find the K.L. I found. Then perhaps you can, like me, smile indulgently at the migrants, knowing in your heart that not only is it a great place to visit, it is also worth the stay.

Shoba Devan

The Founding Of Kuala Lumpur

Kuala Lumpur was never the centre of an ancient culture or civilisation. No philosophers, no scientists, no generals can lay claim to its inspiration. Indeed, just 100 years ago, it was nothing more than marsh, muck and mudbank.

In 1857, an expedition of Chinese tin miners headed up the Klang River from Pengkalan Batu (now Port Klang), then the capital of the Sultanate of Selangor. They were prospecting for tin, a mineral that commanded the kind of attention that is reserved for oil these days. After several days, they arrived at the confluence of the Klang and Gombak Rivers, where they had to stop, the rivers being too shallow to accommodate their fully-laden flotilla. There was nothing more there than a tiny hamlet nestled in a quagmire of mud. Disgusted, the miners called the place Kuala Lumpur – literally meaning "muddy confluence".

Tin was eventually found in Ampang, upstream of Kuala Lumpur, but because of the shallowness of the rivers, direct access to the minefields was limited. Kuala Lumpur thus became a convenient staging point, where supplies and ore could be brought in or sent out. Buoyed by high tin prices, Kuala Lumpur had developed into a flourishing village by the 1860s. Chinese labour was imported by the thousands to man the mines that had opened up its hinterland.

The imposing Sultan Abdul Samad building

There were some Malays – mainly Bugis traders – but the Chinese immigrants began to dominate. Soon, Kuala Lumpur began to acquire all the characteristics of a booming mining town – seedy brothels, gambling dens and organised crime.

Selangor's aristocrats did not interfere with this development initially. They were content to collect export duties from the mined ore. They left the control of the Chinese immigrant population largely in the hands of a community leader called "Kapitan China". The most

The minaret-shaped tower of the Railway Station

illustrious Kapitan was Yap Ah Loy. A Hakka immigrant who came to the country at only 17, his tenure of office from 1868 till 1885 proved to be the most momentous in Kuala Lumpur's history.

Kuala Lumpur's prominence grew. In 1867, Selangor was driven by civil war. The real bone of contention was the right to collect export duties on tin. Initially, the civil war focused on gaining control of forts at the river estuaries where the Malay royalty was based. Kuala Lumpur's miners, fearing the civil war, shipped their ore through whatever river route was open to them. It was perhaps this possibility of tin evading control that caused the protagonists in the civil war to move to Kuala Lumpur.

Yap Ah Loy allied himself with Tengku Kudin, the Viceroy of Selangor. His enemies were led by Syed Hashor, a determined and resourceful man who, enlisting the help of other Malay chiefs, over-ran Kuala Lumpur in August 1872, razing it to the ground. In 1873, Tengku Kudin, with the help of Malay forces from Pahang, won the devastated town back.

Yap Ah Loy is credited for ensuring that K.L. did not disappear back into the marsh. After the war, the town was ruined, tin prices had plunged and the Chinese immigrants were ready to pack up. Yap borrowed to redevelop, cajoled to inspire confidence. Five years later, the strategy paid off as the tin prices soared. In 1879, a British official was, for the first time, sent to live in Kuala Lumpur. In 1880, Selangor moved its capital to the muddy confluence.

The next major personality in the city's history was Frank Swettenham, the Resident of Selangor, who was appointed in 1882. Swettenham tore down the shanties and lean-tos that formed much of K.L. then and replaced them with brick structures. He was responsible for the construction of the K.L.-Klang railway link, ending its dependence on the river.

K.L. continued to grow. An active policy of emigration, the setting aside of reserves and the encouragement of agriculture on its periphery increased the Malay population while diminishing the role of the Chinese migrants. Indian labourers were brought in to work on coffee and rubber estates and on the railroad. The city began to assume its cosmopolitan façade. In 1896, Kuala Lumpur was declared capital of the Federated Malay States. Both world wars did little damage to the city, and in 1957, 100 years after the mining expedition, the campsite qualified as the capital of sovereign Malaya. In 1963, it became capital of Malaysia, and in 1972, it gained city status. Significantly, the city was also wrenched from Selangor and declared a Federal Territory, similar to the status enjoyed by Washington's District of Columbia. In the 18 years since that happened, the city has boomed like never before and now faces all the agonies of a modern day metropolis – traffic-choked streets, air pollution, inadequate public transportation and so on.

Kuala Lumpur today bears no resemblance to the mudpile the Chinese found in 1857. Indeed, the river has been so modified and embanked that a visitor might mistake this for oversize sewers. Much of the city centre however, is faithful to the lines set up by Yap Ah Loy. With some exceptions, Old Market Square and the streets that surround it right up to Chinatown, are remnants of Frank Swettenham's urban renewal efforts.

Deep in prayer at the Jamek Mosque

Polyglot

A visitor to Kuala Lumpur would be justifiably confused by its polyglot population. There are Malays, Chinese, Indians, Eurasians, Portuguese and a lot more that do not become obvious immediately. The various races once occupied different parts of the city, but these days, racially oriented neighbourhoods have become difficult to identify.

The Chinese occupy Chinatown of course, much of nearby Pudu, Sungai Besi and Salak

Jamek mosque strategically located at the confluence of the Batu and Gombak rivers

South areas. They are mainly Cantonese, though a fair amount of Hokkiens are also found. The Chinese are mainly Taoists and Buddhists, though a substantial number are Christians.

The Malays have tended to congregate in the Kampung Baru, Kampung Datuk Keramat, Ulu Kelang, Ampang and Sungai Pencala areas. Though a few trace their families back to Swettenham's time, the vast majority are recent arrivals. All are devout Muslims and the profusion of mosques, particularly in Malay neighbourhoods, attest to this.

The Indian neighbourhoods are mainly in the Jalan Tun Sambanthan and Sentul areas. Their presence there is related to the fact that Malayan Railway maintained institutional housing for their labourers in these areas. Most of the Indians were South Indians, but a fair sprinkling of others – notably the Punjabis, Sindhis and Gujeratis – also came over, mainly as professionals or businessmen. Sri Lankan Tamils were also imported by the Colonial authorities as administrative and clerical staff. Indians are mainly Hindu, though there is a very prominent Indian Muslim community in Kuala Lumpur.

The kaleidoscopic nature of Kuala Lumpur society has given rise to a perplexing host of social norms, some of which apply to only one community. It is traditional, for example, to remove your footwear before entering the house of a Malay or Indian. The Chinese did not have this tradition, but many now follow it. Showing your foot to anybody is considered an insult. Among Malays, it is considered impolite to converse in a loud and raucous manner. Indians and Chinese are not too sensitive about this. The list goes on. There are a number of books on handling culture shock in K.L. (believe me, it does take a book). However, when in doubt, ask. Most K.L. people are friendly and will not hesitate to help out a foreigner struggling in their midst.

HISTORY

1403: Malacca Sultanate begins when Parameswara flees from Sumatra to Malacca.

1303: Advent of Islam in the country.

1857: Kuala Lumpur is founded.

1868: Yap Ah Loy becomes Kapitan China of Kuala Lumpur, develops the town and contributes significantly to K.L.'s history during his tenure of office, which ends in 1885.

1882: Frank Swettenham is appointed Resident of Selangor.

1895: Formation of the Federated Malay States, namely Perak, Pahang, Selangor and Negri Sembilan. The unfederated Malay states are Perlis, Kedah, Kelantan, Trengganu and Johore. Penang, Malacca and Singapore are Straits Settlements.

1896: Kuala Lumpur is declared capital of the Federated Malay States.

1941: The Japanese invasion commences on December 8.

1946: Rise of Malay nationalism. United Malays National Organisation (UMNO) is formed on March 1.

1957: On August 31, Malaya becomes an independent nation, with Tuanku Abdul Rahman as its first Prime Minister. Kuala Lumpur is made the capital of sovereign Malaya.

1963: On September 16, Singapore, Sabah and Sarawak join Malaysia and K.L. becomes the national capital.

1965: Singapore withdraws from Malaysia to become a republic.

1970: Tun Abdul Razak succeeds Tuanku Abdul Rahman as Malaysia's second Prime Minister.

1972: Kuala Lumpur is accorded city status.

1975: Tun Hussein Onn takes over as Prime Minister upon the death of Tun Razak.

1981: Datuk Seri Dr Mahathir Mohamad becomes Malaysia's fourth Prime Minister.

Right, Sultan Abdul Samad building

Day itineraries

For your first three days in Kuala Lumpur, get an insight into the three main facets of the city's cosmopolitan face. The first itinerary allows you to appreciate K.L.'s origins and history; the second, its present role as an exuberant marketplace; and the third, its demure and quiet side, ensconced in greenery and quietude.

Day 1

Getting To Know Kuala Lumpur

A walk and breakfast at Market Square; Wisma Batek; Moresque Government buildings; chicken rice lunch at Government Servants' Club; Infokraf; Menara Dayabumi; National Mosque; Railway Administration Building; Railway Station; dinner at Central Market.

This tour is designed to give you a feel of the city, from its origins as a colonial outpost to a congested metropolis. Start the day with a breakfast of steamed (yes, steamed) bread and *kaya* (a jam of coconut and eggs) at the **Sin Seng Nam Restaurant** at **Medan Pasar Lama**. The square is one of the oldest parts of K.L., its Georgio-Romanesque fa-çades resplendent, if somewhat incongruous, in the morning sun.

After breakfast, walk down the square towards the 12-storey Hong Kong Bank Building (opposite the Bank of Tokyo) and

Map labels:
400 m/ 0.25 miles
St. Mary's Church
Wisma Batek
Jame Mosque
Jalan Tun
J. Gereja
Selangor Club
Sultan Abdul Samad Bldg.
Bukit
Merdeka Square
Jalan Raja
Sin Seng Nam
Start
Govt. Offices
Jalan
K.L. Memorial Library
Lebuh Pasar Besar
Infocraft
Silang
Aman
Tun Perak
Govt. Offices
Menara Dayabumi
Central Market
Jalan Tugu
Jalan
Cheng
Lock
Chenders an
Jalan Sultan Hishamuddin
Sungai Tun
Jalan Kasturi
J. Hang
Hang Lekir
Jalan Sultan
Lembah
General Post Office
Sungai
J. Cheng Hang
J. Sultan Mohamed
Malaya Hotel
National Mosque
Hindu Temple
Jalan Sultan
Peraling
Perdana
Bus Stn.
Tun H S Lee
Jalan
Sikh Temple
Railway Administration Building
Govt. Offices
Jln. Kinabalu
Kuala Lumpur Visitors Centre
Railway Stn.
Public Bank
Chinese Temple

Lush greenery of the Padang leads to the impressive Sultan Abdul Samad building

turn left. You are now at **Jalan Benteng**, and can clearly see the confluence of two rivers – the **Gombak** and **Klang** – that gives the city its name. ("Kuala Lumpur" quite unflatteringly means "muddy confluence").

Head along Jalan Benteng till you reach **Jalan Tun Perak**, then turn left and cross the bridge. On your left is the entrance to **Masjid Jame** (Jame Mosque), a sprawl of spires that is K.L.'s oldest mosque. The rear side of the mosque features a small plaza with that muddy confluence as a backdrop – a place popular with shutterbugs.

Out of the mosque and back down Jalan Tun Perak, go towards **Wisma Batek**, the city's premier *batik* centre, a 12-storey structure. If you appreciate handpainted *batik*, this place alone would have made your walk worthwhile. There is a lot to choose from and they are all lovingly handpainted, not mechanically churned out on a computer-controlled loom.

Detail of fountain at Merdeka Square

Further down, along the same side as Wisma Batek, you will come to K.L.'s most regal neighbourhood. In Moorish majesty, this block of colonial buildings, more than any other landmark, has become representative of Kuala Lumpur. The building facing Jalan Tun Perak once housed the Information Department. It is now being renovated to accommodate courtrooms. Turn left at the junction with **Jalan Raja** and continue down past the bridge. The massive structure you see on the left is the **Bangunan Sultan Abdul Samad** (Sultan Abdul Samad Building). It is not open to the public, so you will have to satisfy yourself with the façade.

The national flag fluttering high

Directly opposite is an open field (the *padang*) fringed by a wooden Tudor-style building on one side and a massive concrete plaza on the other.

The cluster of wooden buildings is another colonial relic, the **Selangor Club**, which prides itself on an ambience that Somerset Maugham would have been comfortable in, as indeed he was. That massive plaza, on the other hand, is the **Merdeka Square**, the symbol of the country's independence.

Cross the *padang* to the other side of Merdeka Square. Just across the road, you will find a nondescript wooden building with the sign **Kelab Kakitangan Kerajaan** (Government Servants' Club). It is no Ritz, but the food is good and the beer cheap. Its chicken rice is reputed to be among the best in Kuala Lumpur.

After lunch, amble down the road to the junction of Jalan Raja and **Lebuh Pasar Besar**. On the right are more colonial buildings, one of which houses the K.L. Memorial Library.

When you reach the junction, cross over to the other side. You are now at **Infokraf** (Infocraft), the closest thing to a handicraft museum in the city.

Further down the same avenue is the gleaming white **Menara Dayabumi** (Dayabumi Complex). Essentially an office building occupied by the national oil

A monument preserved – the Kuala Lumpur Railway Station

company, Petronas, it comes with an unexciting shopping mall. Stop here for a drink and cool off in the air-conditioning. Head left about 50 metres (165 ft) from Dayabumi's entrance towards the General Post Office (Pejabat Pos Besar). Take the underground pedestrian walkway that leads to the other side of the road and on surfacing, head down the same direction as before. Within seconds, the magnificent **Masjid Negara** (National Mosque) with its tall minaret (all 73 metres [240 ft] of it) and geometric lattice-work looms ahead. Resplendent in white marble offset by pools of gurgling water, the mosque accommodates up to 10,000 faithful at any one time. If you wish to enter the mosque, remove your shoes and use the robe provided. Tour the interior where you will see the ornamental pools, fountains, a gallery, the library and the Grand Prayer Hall. Tourists are however forbidden entry to the Prayer Hall. Visiting hours: 9 a.m. to 6 p.m. Saturday through Thursday, 2.45 p.m. to 6 p.m. on Friday. Admission is free.

The **Railway Administration Building**, bulging with domes, is right behind the mosque. Walk around the building to the front. Another Moresque extravagance, the **Kuala Lumpur Railway Station,** is just across the boulevard. The building is K.L.'s proud testimony to architectural preservation. Originally built in 1885, it was rebuilt at the turn of the century and recently refurbished. Again, take the underground pedestrian tunnel to the railway station amd prepare to cross over to Jalan Tun Tan Cheng Lock. The ticketing concourse is air-conditioned and equipped incongruously with plastic chairs and vending machines. After that

Infokraf

Shop for souvenirs in Central Market

walk, both would be more than welcome respite. To enter the platform area, you will have to buy a ticket which costs M20 cents. The tickets are issued by two ancient wall-mounted dispensers near the platform doors. Remember to retain your ticket since it will be collected on the way out. You will now be standing on Platform 1. Walk down to your left for about 10 metres (33 ft) till you reach yet another underground walkway running under the tracks to the other three platforms. Head for Platform 4, then walk out.

You will now be facing **Jalan Tun Tan Cheng Lock**. By this time, the day's heat would have taken its toll, so be good to yourself and hail a taxi to the **Central Market**. This was once K.L.'s largest wet market, but was converted a few years ago into a cultural-cum-shopping mall. There is an immense variety of merchandise sold here, including exotic handicraft and art. You can have your portrait painted, have glass sculptures custom-made to your personal design, get your shoe fixed while you wait or sample Indian curry powders. Often, cultural shows are held in the evenings, with free admission.

Outdoors is a pedestrian mall that fronts ancient-looking shops that peddle dried fish, rice wine and porcelain Taoist icons.

Dinner is recommended at the **Riverbank**, a small restaurant in the Central Market itself, that serves continental food and entertains with live jazz music.

Wear a piece of culture!

Chinatown

Coin museum in Menara Maybank; bak-ku-teh at Jalan Hang Lekir; walk down Petaling Street; Chinese vegetarian lunch at Jalan Panggong; visit Hindu and Chinese temples; seafood dinner and cultural show at Lake Titiwangsa.

Chinatown in Kuala Lumpur is similar to Chinatowns everywhere else (except perhaps China) – a confusion of cacophony and colour. Start the day staid, however, by visiting the **Muzium Numismatik** (Numismatic Museum), country's only coin museum at the ground floor of the **Maybank** (Malayan Banking Building) on **Jalan Tun Perak** (opening hours are 10 a.m. to 6 p.m.). Towering ominously over the city, the building is, at 51 storeys, one of the tallest high-rises in Kuala Lumpur. Chinatown is right across the roundabout in front of the coin museum. However, the traffic here is horrendous and totally unsympathetic to pedestrians.

A safer way is to keep left on the kerb as you exit the building along Jalan Tun Perak, then head towards the pedestrian bridge fronting **Hentian Puduraya** (Puduraya Bus Station) about 500 metres (1,650 ft) away. Climb the bridge into the bus station and walk to the pedestrian bridge on the other side of the building. Head down to the kerb and towards **Jalan Tun Tan Cheng Lock**. Before long, you will come across **Jalan Sultan**, which marks the beginning of Chinatown.

Actually, Chinatown K.L. consists of two more streets parallel to Jalan Sultan – Jalan Petaling and Jalan Tun H S Lee, and one more perpendicular to it, Jalan Hang Lekir. Go down Jalan Sultan past Rex Cinema and turn right into **Jalan Hang Lekir**.

This street is lined with shops selling meat floss and other exotic edibles. Stop over at the **Futo House of Curry Laksa**. and have a typical Chinese breakfast (rather, brunch, by this time) of *bak-ku-*

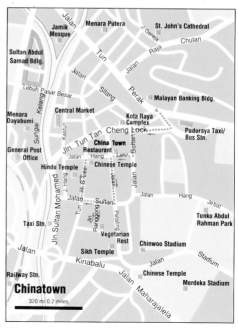

Mooncakes a treat for a sweet tooth – only in September

teh, a fragrant stew of pork ribs and herbs. If something more *kosher (halal)* is up your alley, then sit down to an equally unusual repast of steamed bread and coffee.

Just down the street, Jalan Hang Lekir meets Jalan Petaling. If that sounds like the roll call for a wrestling match, you are not far off. Jalan Petaling is not simply chaotic, it is pure anarchy. Along this narrow ribbon of asphalt, sidewalk vendors compete avariciously with the stream of vehicles in front of them and flanks of shops behind. Shopping in this nightmare can be exacting.

There are a couple of things you should know about shopping along Jalan Petaling. First, to get the best price, bargain enthusiastically. Second, despite whatever you are told, Jalan Petaling is not the place for designer labels. You may see vendors hawking Gucci handbags and Cartier watches, but both have not yet given out sidewalk franchises.

To get to your lunch spot, walk down **Jalan Petaling** towards Jalan Sultan. Turn right at **Jalan Sultan** and then turn left into a small alley called **Jalan Panggong** after 50 metres (165 ft). Walk down another 50 metres and you will arrive at the **Wan Fo Yuan Vegetarian Restaurant** where you can try a Chinese vegetarian lunch. Chinese vegetarian cooking is an art form in its own right. The food resembles meat or fish, but is entirely of vegetable origin.

After lunch, turn right and head back to Jalan Sultan. When you get there, turn left and walk towards the junction with **Jalan Tun H S Lee**. Turn right at this junction and you will see the **Sri**

Affluence mix with tradition in Jalan Sultan, Chinatown

At quiet corner at Persatuan Kwong Siew Temple

Mahamariaman Hindu Temple looming up on the left side of the road. Further down on the right side of the road is the **Persatuan Kwong Siew Chinese Temple**. Both are open to the public.

To enter the Hindu temple, however, you are expected to remove your footwear first. Sometimes, flower vendors ply their trade outside the Hindu temple. The flowers are fragrant and are strung together like beads. The floral garlands are sold by the length. Buy a strand and drape it around your neck. Its refreshing scent banishes the mugginess of the afternoon heat. After the Chinese temple, hail a taxi along **Jalan Hang Lekir** for your ride back to the hotel. It is time for a shower and to contemplate dinner.

For dinner, tell the taxi driver to take you to **Restoran TT Wangsa** (TT Wangsa Restaurant). This is a floating restaurant located in the Titiwangsa Lake Gardens, off **Jalan Kuantan**. The speciality here is Cantonese-style seafood. Try the steamed sea bass with ginger. The live cultural shows add a rustic touch to the day.

Quaint and Quiet

Morning stroll in Lake Gardens; visit the deer park; hibiscus and orchid gardens; National Monument; banana leaf-plate lunch; National Museum and Art Gallery; dinner at an open-air hawker centre in Jalan Alor.

Gateway to Sri Mahamariaman Hindu Temple

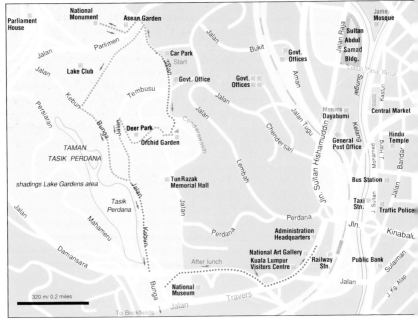

Alfred Venning was a man obsessed. The former state treasurer was more taken with the idea of a botanical garden in the heart of K.L than with greenbacks. He succeeded eventually. Now, 100 years later, the name Venning scarcely means anything to the people of

K.L., but his legacy strikes deep in the hearts of many. The **Lake Gardens**, started by Venning, with its 104 hectares (257 acres) of close-cropped lawns, undulating hillocks and carefully cultivated gardens, is a sanctuary from the maddening mayhem of the city. It also forms the core

The Deer Park – a treat for the children

of K.L.'s green lung programme. With five public parks covering a total of 218½ hectares (537 acres), City Hall realises the burgeoning metropolis will require more green belts and has earmarked about 1,800 hectares (4448 acres) for 12 more parks by the year 2,000.

Get an early start today. The gardens are at their best in the cool of the morning or the evening. Tell the taxi driver to take you to **Taman Tasik Perdana**. Get off just before the car park at the intersection of Jalan Cenderawasih and Jalan Tanglin. Head down a stoned pathway across the road that leads to the boathouse which is located right next to the lake. There is a convenient shuttle service around the park and the ride is pleasant, with stops at all the attractions. If you prefer a stroll, it is 20 minutes from the lake to the deer park and popular orchid gardens.

To get your bearings right, read the signs prominently placed

outside the boathouse and the maps displayed along the footpaths. They give very clear directions and lead you to the Deer Park and Orchid Gardens safely, where you can see species of doe, hind and fawn, as well as the smallest deer, the mousedeer. You can also feast your eyes on the luxuriant array of hundreds of orchid species and hybrids.

If walking is not your cup of tea, then take the shuttle, get off at the relevant stops and catch it when it comes around again. The shuttle begins at 8.30 a.m. and runs every 30 minutes till 6.30 p.m. Vending machines at the various stops will keep your thirst quenched. For snacks, there is a restaurant located near the carpark. As you face the lake, head down right along Jalan Kebun Bunga till you come to the carpark. The restaurant is adjacent to it and sells sandwiches and pastries.

When you have had your fill of green, backtrack to **Jalan Cenderawasih** – this is the road where you started. Jalan Parlimen is perpendicular to Jalan Cenderawasih on

Serenity at the Lake Gardens

An impressive salutation, the National Monument

the left. Opposite Jalan Parlimen is the **National Monument**. It is worth a look for its fine sculpturing and bronzework and while you are there, you will see the **Asean Garden** featuring the region's finest works of art. (Asean is a grouping of the following countries: Singapore, Malaysia, Indonesia, Thailand, the Philippines and Brunei).

You would have worked up a hearty appetite by now and since it is around midday, hail a cab to **Brickfields**, just 2 km (1.25 miles) or a 10-minute ride away.

Try a typical South Indian lunch, eaten off a banana leaf, at the **Sri Devi Restaurant** on **Jalan Travers**. You have a choice of plain steamed rice or *beryani* (fragrant rice), or *thosai* (flour based pancakes). In true South Indian style, meals are normally eaten with the fingers, but ask for cutlery if you are not comfortable doing so. The waiters will tour tables with buckets of lentil gravy and well-cooked vegetables, which they will serve in generous dollops. You also have a variety of meat dishes to choose from.

Ask for yogurt to go with the meal; together with the air-conditioning, it will help cool the body after the morning heat. Indulge in dessert of typical Indian sweetmeats such as *jelebi*, *mysore pak* or *ladu*, but dieters be warned that they are all sugar and milk. For this full meal, you need only spend between M$2.50 and M$4.50.

From Brickfields, take a cab to the **Muzium Negara** (National Museum) – the fare should be around M$2. Spend a couple of hours soaking up Malaysian history and culture.

National Art Gallery

Historical mural, National Museum

huge murals in Italian glass. The offbeat museum exhibits of cats and skulls, to treasures from the grave can be attributed to the retired museum curator Datuk Sharum Yub. (Note that photography is prohibited here). The museum is small enough not to require a guided tour, so wander from room to room. Daily operating hours are from 9 a.m. to 6 p.m. and admission is free.

If you get a little hungry, stalls at the car park sell drinks and snacks. After you've had your fill, leave via the car park and head left towards the spires of the K.L. Railway Station.

You will see the **National Art Gallery** at the back, once the former Majestic Hotel, which lived up to its name during its time. In 1983, the hotel was converted into the art gallery. There is still a regal dignity about the place and it is an appropriate venue for works of top Malaysian artists. Permanent collections of artists' work are displayed on the ground to the third floors, with 35 rooms in all. At the gallery, exhibits range from *batik*, wall paintings to wood sculptures. The annex to the right of the gallery is the creative centre, where exhibitions by local and foreign artists are held throughout the year. Gallery opening hours: daily from 10 a.m. to 6 p.m., except Fridays, when it opens from noon to 3 p.m. Admission is free.

In the evening, go to **Jalan Alor** off **Jalan Bukit Bintang** for dinner (refer to Bukit Bintang Walk in the Pick and Choose Chapter). By 6.30 or 7 p.m., food stalls will have sprouted down the entire length of the street, selling all varieties of local food. This is a great place to sample hawker fare from the breadth and length of the country. The row of stalls at Penang Corner, diagonally across the Love Valley social escort service, offer specialities from Penang: *char kway teow* (broad, flat rice noodles fried with meat and bean sprouts), *mee yoke* (prawn noodles), *lobak* (mixed cold meats), *oh-luak* (fried oyster omelette) and *ikan panggang* (grilled fish). The prawn noodles and *char kway teow* in particular, are said to come close to the reputed and authentic stalls in Penang.

After dinner, stroll along **Jalan Hicks**, which is perpendicular to Jalan Alor. All forms of vendors market their wares here, from out of season durians to traditional medicine and dog shows. The Bukit Bintang area is the hub of entertainment after sundown. It used to have the wild west sort of nightlife – girlie bars, striptease and peep machines. Although the area is comparatively sanitised today, some of the "action" still exists – in the form of massage parlours, nightclubs and discos. Taxis are available round the clock, so you do not have to worry about transportation back to your hotel if you wish to nurse your drink through the wee hours of the morning.

Pick & Choose

The following half-day itineraries are tailored to time-frames of five to six hours each, allowing for pleasant shopping, laid-back viewing and anything else that may come to mind. These little tours should open windows on life in K.L. – from the harried hustle of Chinatown to the sedate placidity of Kampung Baru. You will find a microcosm of Malaysian life amply represented here. Note that it can get awfully hot after 10 in the morning right up till 5 in the evening, the average humidity in the mid-90s. So keep to the shade and consume lots of water.

A.M. Itineraries

1. Bukit Bintang Walk

Karyaneka handicraft village; walkabout in Bukit Bintang; shopping; Chinese vegetarian lunch.
This tour is basically a jaunt through Kuala Lumpur's most prestigious shopping area and while it is listed as a half-day tour, you may, if you are a shopping buff, end up stretching it to a couple of

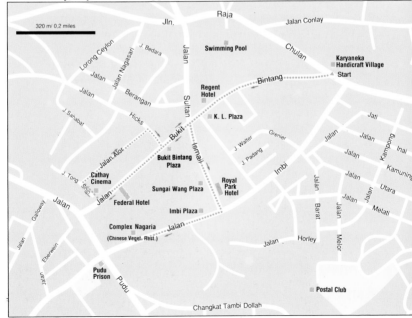

Busy street on Bukit Bintang

days. A tip on how to handle this neighbourhood – browse quickly through the handicraft village, malls and shops, then zoom in on your favourite after lunch.

Begin the morning at **Karyaneka**, a cluster of wooden buildings nestled in an old colonial neighbourhood along **Jalan Raja Chulan**. Built by the Malaysian Handicraft Board, each of the buildings at Karyaneka reflect the dominant architecture found in Malaysia's 13 states. There are a total of 14 buildings, including a showroom and shop. The display of handicraft within each building is similarly thematic. You can browse among kites and tops from Kelantan, *batik* and *songket* from Trengganu and pottery from Sarawak. The prices are not exactly cheap (Karyaneka was set up on the premise that it would be frequented only by rich tourists), but the variety is staggering. The displays change all the time, depending on the availability of a particular line of handicraft. Even if you do not pick up a souvenir or two, you can watch craftsmen at work here. The handicraft centre closes by 6 p.m. There is also a small ethno-botanical garden and an international craft museum on the premises.

Karyaneka Handicraft Centre

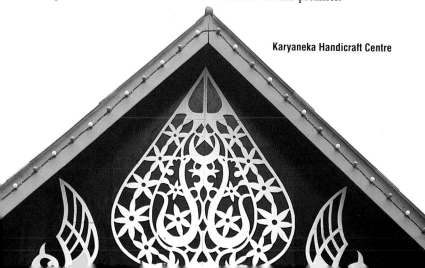

Kites from Kelantan – a feast for the eyes

As you make your way out, keep left. The junction opposite the exit of Karyaneka marks the beginning of **Jalan Bukit Bintang**. Cross over and head up the road (about 500 metres [0.3 miles]) till you see **K.L. Plaza** on the left and on the right, the brand new **Regent of Kuala Lumpur**, opened in November 1989. The hotel's doorways are stunning, edged with gleaming stainless steel and embossed with a brass *kris*, the traditional Malay double edged dagger. The lobby, designed to create a feeling of spaciousness, is impressive with its high ceilings and water falling softly down marble steps lined with beds of brilliantly coloured flowers. Cool off over a drink at the hotel's coffee house.

Back on the street, turn right and keep going till you reach the traffic lights. You are now in the heart of Bukit Bintang. You could shop till you drop here, at the twin shopping centres of **Sungai Wang Plaza** and **Bukit Bintang Plaza, Lot 10, K.L. Plaza** which you passed earlier, and a myriad of shops lining the streets. Both Sungai Wang (which you will visit later) and Bukit Bintang Plaza, which are about 20 metres (65 ft) left of the traffic lights, boast of massive department stores.

Sungai Wang's anchor tenant is Parkson Grand, while the upmarket Metrojaya dominates Bukit Bintang Plaza. In the K.L. Plaza, look out for Mun Loong. All three are very reputable establishments and have a broad merchandise spread. Nonetheless, the real strength of these stores or, for that matter, most of the stores in this area, is in clothing. There are all manner of clothes available, from designer labels to the more moderately priced apparel.

There are also a lot of shops selling shoes, belts, handbags and other accessories to go with

Traditional architecture kept alive – the Tourist Information Centre

the fashionable garments. Both Metrojaya and Mun Loong have a very extensive range of cosmetic and personal toiletries, most carrying exotic French names that lend an aura of mystery and romance (besides a hefty price tag) to the product. Cosmetics in Malaysia are duty-free however, and these stores probably charge lower than in duty-free stores.

Bukit Bintang's shopping delights do not stop at clothing. In all the malls mentioned above, there are shops selling a whole lot of other goods, from watches to fast food to photographic equipment to books. The prices are reasonable as the area is frequented by a substantial local crowd and competition among retailers is stiff. Sungai Wang in particular, can get very crowded, especially during major festival periods. Both the K.L. Plaza and the Sungai Wang feature cultural shows and music performances on occasion. To find out the programmes and schedules, check with the information desk that fronts each mall.

After you have finished shopping at Bukit Bintang Plaza, turn left at the main entrance and head down Jalan Bukit Bintang. In stark contrast to the malls you just visited, the stores that front the boulevard are unexciting and do not offer as wide a range of merchandise. Most are just offices, while others are unabashed tourist traps.

Keep walking and 500 metres (0.3 miles) further down, you will come to the Federal Hotel. Then cross the road to the Cathay Cinema. Head down behind the cinema and you are in **Jalan Alor**. Keeping to the right side of the road, head down this street. There are hair dressing salons, travel agencies and numerous shops selling a variety of goods littered along this route. Walk till you get to the top of the **Jalan Hicks** junction, turn right and you are in Jalan Bukit Bintang again.

If you find this part of Bukit Bintang mundane, rest assured it is only so during the day. This part of Bukit Bintang comes alive after dark and it is strongly recom-

Night lights beckon at Bukit Bintang

mended that you should come back at a later time to sample its sundown delights. Behind placid shop fronts and sanitised fast food outlets lurks another personality – one that comes out with the stars (*bintang* means star). The first sign of this is the garish neons and tell-tale red lights that seem to spring up from every second storey window. Jalan Alor metamorphoses from a congested jam of metal and exhaust fumes into brightly lit chaos of food stalls selling a whole range of Chinese cuisine, from the mundane to the exotic –

venison, tripe and even dog meat – for prices beginning at M$3.

Cross the road and turn left. You will immediately see the traffic lights as you do so. At the junction, turn right and head down **Jalan Sultan Ismail**. Keep to the right side of the road. About a block away from Sungai Wang Plaza is **Imbi Plaza**, K.L.'s computer mall. All three floors are occupied by shops selling the latest in software and hardware. In particular, you may want to look at the locally fabricated IBM clones on sale. Malaysia is the world's largest exporter of semi-conductor devices, and obtaining chips is a cinch. A fully built-up IBM AT facsimile, complete with colour monitor, costs only around M$2,200.

Right next door to the Imbi Plaza is the **Melia Kuala Lumpur**. Here, you can get an aerial view of Kuala Lumpur if you take a ride up the hotel's bubble lift to the 18th floor. Next to the hotel is the **Complex Nagaria**, in which is a Chinese vegetarian restaurant called **Pure Mind**, located on the ground floor. You can spot the restaurant's sign board from street level. Operating hours are 11 a.m.-3 p.m. and 6-10 p.m. The food here is delicious, though pricey. Munch on fried lotus root or a yam basket. If you are undecided what to pick, just ask the waiter for his recommendations. Enjoy a wholesome meal while you contemplate your shopping plans for the rest of the day.

2. Kampung Baru Walk

A tour of the oldest Malay settlement; visit a Sikh temple; a mosque; browse through a Malay bazaar.

This tour takes you around the oldest Malay settlement in Kuala

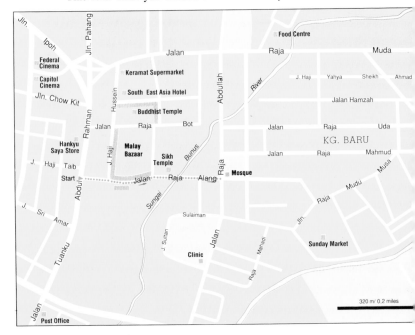

Mouth-watering bananas

Lumpur – **Kampung Baru** (founded in 1899), which is a real contrast to Chinatown. It is far more sedate, the din decibels away in the bedlam of **Jalan Petaling**. It is still interesting, though you will not find the merchandise spread of Chinatown's sidewalk vendors.

Head down **Jalan Raja Alang** from its junction with **Jalan Tuanku Abdul Rahman**. The road is supposedly two-way, for some obscure reason, but the pedestrian holds sway around here. As you walk down Jalan Raja Alang, patronise the fruit stalls on the left. In addition to the regular apple and orange fare, some of them specialise in exotic tropical fruits that never see the light of a supermarket shelf. Depending on the season, you might find durians, mangosteens, rambutans, mangoes, and pineapples, among others.

Further down, there is a municipal hawker food emporium, **Pusat Penjaja Dewan Bandaraya**, where Malay ethnic food is served. Try the *mee jawa* or *mee soup*, both noodle-based dishes, for breakfast, before continuing your journey. A meal costs between M$2 and M$5.

One would have thought that a Sikh temple would be out of place in a largely Muslim neighbourhood, yet there it stands in red brick glory to the left of the road, further down from the Pusat Penjaja food centre. Its façade is reminiscent of pre-war shophouses in K.L. The temple gates are normally closed to vehicular traffic, but there is a side entrance that allows individuals to enter. In consonance with the Sikh faith, there are no icons, but pictures of Sikh saints line the entrance hall. The temple is open only on occasion, so you may have to satisfy yourself with a view through the gates.

Prominently red, the Kampung Baru Sikh Temple

Head straight down till Jalan Raja Alang meets **Jalan Raja Abdullah**. Just across the crossroads is the **Kampung Baru**

Kampung Baru Mosque

Mosque, built around 1924, one of the first concrete structures to be erected in the quarter. Indeed, the charm of Kampung Baru lies in the architecture and layout of its houses. Typically made of wood, the houses are spacious and high-ceilinged, in keeping with Malay architectural tradition. Often, prayer mats or religious writing grace the door, underscoring the intense devotion the Muslims have for their religion.

Houses like these line the stretch of Jalan Raja Alang beyond the mosque, though much has been sacrificed to the clinical efficiency of modern-day office block structures. The residents do not normally open their homes to the public. However, on the rare occasion, it

Muslim caps – a call for prayer

may be possible to gain privileged entry, depending on the circumstances and predisposition of the occupants.

The end of the road terminates in a row of shophouses and a mini-bazaar. Here, you can indulge in more ethnic cooking and the variety is really breathtaking. Visit the local jewellery shop. Malay goldsmiths employ very different patterns compared with their Indian or Chinese counterparts. Finally, it is an excellent place to hail a taxi back, in case the prospect of walking becomes too daunting.

One thing though – avoid this tour in the day during the fasting month of Ramadan. You will find all the eating stalls closed. They only open and serve with a vengeance after 7.30 p.m. – to signal the break of a day's fasting.

3. Batu Caves

Visit Batu Caves; a walk up to the temple cave; visit the centre of Indian art.

This one is sure to awaken your calf muscles and give it a fresh lease of life. No visit to K.L. is complete without a trip to the caves, at once the holiest Hindu shrine, the darling of cave ecologists and geologists and an unabashed tourist trap.

The caves have a lot going for them. They form the southernmost outcrop in the Northern Hemisphere. They are riddled with caves that support a variety of exotic wildlife. The main cave holds a shrine of Lord Subramaniam, a deity revered by the Hindus. Every

Interior of the Batu Caves

year, at a festival called *Thaipusam*, hundreds of thousands converge at the shrine, offering thanksgiving and undertaking unbelievable acts of self-immolation as a sign of their devotion.

Getting there is easy. City taxis service the caves, the fare being in the region of M$7 to M$9, depending on where they are boarded.

The first thing that will strike you as you approach the main gates is the immense concrete staircase that leads up to the temple caves. There are about 250 steps in all, making it quite a climb. Monkeys perch in perfect nonchalance along the staircase, and will quite willingly accept bananas (or for that matter, just about anything else) in mock humility. You can buy fruits and nuts to feed the monkeys at food stalls near the row of shops to the right of the staircase. These monkeys are not tame enough to be held or fondled, though, and a comfortable distance is well advised.

Once inside the main cave, take care to observe religious sensitivities by avoiding actions that are socially offensive. There are a few grottos in the cave, and some attention to this matter is necessary. Climb down the 250 steps and once back on the ground, you may want to visit the **Gallery of Indian Art**, located to the left of the staircase. Set in another

37

Mythological thrives in the Gallery of Indian Art

cave, it features clay figurines from Indian mythological themes. True to the art form, the sculptures of Indian deities and scenes from Indian mythology are realistic with heavy accent on bright, garish, colour schemes.

There are a few shops you may want to browse through while waiting for the jelly below your knee to congeal back into muscle. There are a couple of souvenir shops, but besides the "I was at Batu Caves" pendants (M$3 to M$9 each), there is nothing you cannot get in the city. One shop specialises in fresh coconut water, served if you like, in the nut itself. The others serve mainly Indian ethnic food for M$2 to M$5 per person. One shop specialises in Indian religious paraphernalia such as oil lamps, camphor holders, incense holders and icons. Depending on your predisposition, this shop can be a collector's paradise.

4. Agriculture Park

A trip to the Agriculture Park and a visit to the Sultan Salahuddin Mosque in Shah Alam; bring a packed meal and drinks for the day; fishing enthusiasts should also bring their own gear.

This tour is definitely for those into greenery. Located just about 30 km (18½ miles) from Kuala Lumpur, the **Agriculture Park** is a living testimony to Malaysian agriculture. Carved out of 900 hectares (2,224 acres) of tropical forest, the park features many facets of the local crop, livestock and fisheries, in an ambience that is hard to beat for rusticity. To get there, take a taxi from the Klang Bus Station at **Jalan Sultan Mohamed** and ask the driver to take you to **Taman Pertanian Malaysia, Shah Alam**. The transport links to the park are not too well developed at present, so it may be prudent to negotiate with the taxi driver to pick you up as well. The two-way fare should be around M$12 per person.

Within the park itself, the favoured means of transport is walking or cycling. Bicycles can be rented at the gate for M50 cents each, no time limit. A bus shuttle operates on weekends, the fare being M50 cents. From the gate, it is only a short walk to the park administration building where you can pile up literature on present and planned facilities.

How to get around in the Agriculture Park

It is also useful to ask for maps to help you get around the area. Maps are also clearly displayed at all shuttle bus shelters in the park.

Begin your tour at the wild fruit orchard, located right behind the administration building. It has been planted with exotic species such as the durian, mangosteen and rambutan trees. These are not fruiting yet and you have to be satisfied with this canopy of dense boughs and dried branches. Right across the road from the orchard is the rice garden and rice milling plant. They are models of the quintessential rice paddies that so dominate Asian countrysides.

Climb the hill behind the milling plant, walk through the cocoa estate, and you arrive at the fisheries lake. Besides the breathtaking scenery, fishing is also possible, even encouraged. However, you have to bring your own gear. At this point, patronise the bottle-shaped milk stand next to the lake. In addition to a range of flavoured milks, you can also buy the local yogurt, *dadih*, a sweet, jelly-like variety which originated in the state of Kedah.

There are other attractions, of course, notably the deer park, aviary, fish cages, spice and beverage, orchid and flower gardens, but they are a sweaty hike or ride away and would take up most part of the day. Just follow the maps at the bus shelters, or those you might have collected at the administration building. The route

Rice fields

Nutritious milk awaits the hungry visitor

can be convoluted, the roads meandering to avoid felling large trees. If this type of hike appeals to you, then along the way, you might also like to visit the **Air Kuning** and **Sungai Baru Lakes**.

Air Kuning Lake is located in the midst of a tropical forest stretch. It allows for some fishing but the main attraction is the pristine natural environment. There are numerous hiking trails that meander through the forest and all are clearly marked. Sungai Baru Lake features a "cage culture" complex where fish like the telapis, river catfish, sultan fish and other exotics, are reared in floating cages. There is no charge for entering the cage complex area. The scenery is breathtaking as well.

The park is still very new and additional facilities are being built all the time. In construction are an oil palm and rubber estate, chalets and an aquarium fish centre. You would be well advised to make exhaustive enquiries at the administrative centre.

There are no restaurants in the park, so bring along a packed meal, especially if you are planning to stay the day. There are, however, a number of the bottle-shaped milk stands mentioned earlier. If milk is not up your alley, bring along canned or packet drinks.

On the return trip, stop over at the **Sultan Salahuddin Mosque** at Shah Alam, which is along the way. The blue-tinted dome of the mosque is the most prominent structure in the city – the dome is bigger than that of St Paul's in London. Its spire can, in fact, be seen from miles away. The mosque itself is laid out along the same lines as the Great Mosque of Mecca and much of the architecture is contemporary Arabic. When you enter the prayer hall, you will notice the "ceiling fans" which do not hang down from the ceiling at all, but are mounted from stalks from the ground.

The mosque grounds have been very extensively landscaped with gardens and a pool which eventually links up to the Shah Alam lake garden, the suburb's premier green lung. The mosque is relatively new and the saplings have yet to grow into trees.

An art to cultivate – mushroom culture

Standing proudly before the Sultan Salahuddin Mosque, Shah Alam

Before touring the interior of the mosque, remember to remove your footwear.

After this, you may want to head back to your hotel and prepare for dinner. If you had negotiated with the taxi driver for a two-way trip earlier, he will drop you off at the Klang Bus Station Terminus. From here, it is very easy to hail another cab back to your hotel.

5. Zoo and Aquarium Negara

Visit the national zoo and aquarium; see the endangered animal species; lunch at the zoo or at Malay hawker stalls nearby.

Kuala Lumpur's zoological gardens do not compare with San Diego's or London's, but it gives an insight into Malaysia's rich wildlife resources. Both the zoo and the national aquarium are located on the same grounds and you can cover both for the price of one entry ticket. Entry fees are M$4 for adults and M$1 for children while photo fees are M$1.

Most city taxis will take you there for about M$10 – ask for **Zoo Negara, Ulu Kelang**; and catching a cab back should be no problem.

The zoo is located about 15 km (0.9 miles) from the central business district. At one time, it was set amidst virgin jungle and rubber estates. The urban sprawl has caught up with the 25-hectare (62 acres) zoo, however, and today it stands like an oasis in the midst of a concrete desert. Nothing exemplifies that description better than the actual visit. A whiz past petrol bunkers, supermarkets and rows upon rows of houses, up to the entrance with the fast food billboard...then, *voila*...another world!

From the zoo's entry gate, numerous paths meander between

Taking a rest after lunch at the zoo

wooded groves and tree-lined enclaves where the animal enclosures are located. Among the more exotic exhibits are the Sumatran tiger, Malayan tapir, orang utan and the gibbons (the least evolved of all the apes). All are on the endangered list and extremely rare outside this part of the world. Other attractions include the Malayan honey bear and the world's smallest deer, the mousedeer.

In addition to these, you will find the run-of-the-mill zoo fare like giraffes, lions, camels and elephants. The aquarium is located at the back of the zoo proper and also boasts some unusual specimens, such as the Malayan Bony Tongue, Malaysian riverine carps and coral reef fishes. If you go on a weekend, be on the lookout for pickpockets who have been known to take advantage of the crowd because of the subdued lighting at the aquarium.

While the general layout of the zoo is pastoral, even rustic, it does not obviate the visitor from the heat. If you are not up to walking, the zoo provides a shuttle bus that covers most of the exhibits. Still, there are numerous vending machines dispensing canned and packet drinks located strategically along the zoo grounds.

For food, there is only a Kentucky Fried Chicken outlet, though there are a couple of stands that serve ice cream and other snacks. If fast food is not your cup of tea, take a stroll beyond the car park. Adjoining the main road, there is a row of food stalls that serve ethnic Malay food. Besides the culinary variety, it is also an ideal place to hail a cab back to your hotel.

P.M. Itineraries

1. Down Infamous Chow Kit

The Mall and an early dinner at Medan Hang Tuah; a walk down Chow Kit; browse at an open-air bazaar.

Mention **Chow Kit** to any Kuala Lumpurian and watch the sly grin spread over his face. There is a good reason for it. Chow Kit was probably the most notorious neighbourhood in the city at one time. Today, urban renewal has sanitised much of what was once K.L.'s sleaze centre. But old impressions die hard. Besides, such things are not easily suppressed. In the backlanes and dark alleys of the Chow Kit area, transvestites still ply their trade and call girls stare out of masks of cheap make-up. It is not exactly Patpong.

Chow Kit today actually has a chic shopping plaza, **The Mall**, at the end of **Jalan Putra**. Begin your walk from here. The Mall is resplendent in shining glass and concrete, and houses a host of upmarket establishments, including the Japanese retail chain, **Yaohan**. The gleam disappears abruptly on the fourth floor, where almost half the floor area has been dedicated to a theme food court called **Medan Hang Tuah**. It is modelled after K.L. in the 1930s and the builders have painstakingly recreated doorways, street lights and building façades of the period. The food court offers an immense variety of food, mainly Chinese. Have an early dinner here.

After the Mall, head down Jalan Putra towards **Jalan Chow Kit** and then past the cross roads to **Jalan Tuanku Abdul Rahman**. This point marks the beginning of the Chow Kit shopping zone, a bazaar so elaborate that only major landmarks are given.

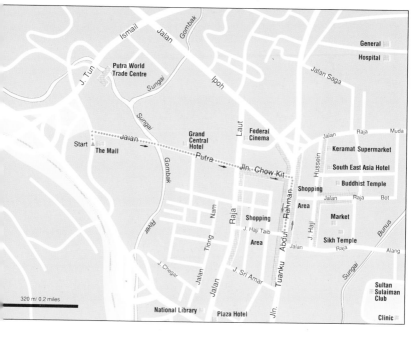

The Mall – for chic shopping

Start on the side of the road you are now on and head down in the direction of the traffic. The shops on the side are crammed with buys and come-ons that would tempt even the most discerning miser.

The sidewalk, in the meantime, becomes noticeably uncomfortable, as vendors open up stalls that sell everything. If you thought you saw some pretty exciting shopping on this side, you are going to go *ga-ga* on the opposite stretch. Continue walking down the road and use the crossing to get over to the other side. The bazaar here occupies (though "congests" is a better word) not only the sidewalks of Jalan Tuanku Abdul Rahman, but the side streets as well. The authorities have long since given up on ensuring vehicular traffic flow, and pedestrians have taken over.

The range of goods is very wide, but like in Chinatown, do not be deceived by contraband designer labels and brands.

Prices are inflated with a view to bargaining, so do not be shy – in fact, be absolutely ruthless; it is not unusual to get discounts of at least 20 percent. There are lots of food for sale, but be wary of unlicensed hawkers.

Shops galore at the Mall

2. Tuanku Abdul Rahman Walk

Lunch at the Coliseum Cafe; wander down Jalan Tuanku Abdul Rahman and explore the Masjid India area; visit Little India; enjoy a dinner of North Indian cuisine.

Built in 1928, the **Coliseum Cafe** located next to the Coliseum Cinema on **Jalan Tuanku Abdul Rahman** has definitely seen better days. Its shabby decor and mismatched furniture and fittings belie a time when the place was a popular hangout with the white planter, tin miner and trader. It serves a tasty chicken chop, and fish and chips though. Start your tour with lunch here, where you can get a good meal for between M$10 and M$20.

A relic of early Kuala Lumpur, the cafe's façade has been maintained and provides sharp contrast to the fast food joints down the same block, making it the ideal start of a tour that blends the antiquity of K.L. with its 20th-century slickness.

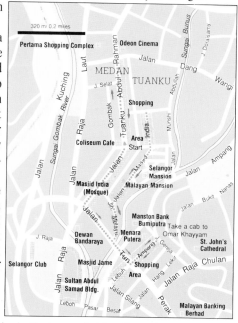

After lunch, join the hundreds on the pavements of **Jalan Tuanku Abdul Rahman**, the city's longest shopping street named after the first King of independent Malaysia. Merchandise from textiles and carpets to shoes and leather goods are hawked by both shop and sidewalk vendors.

To thoroughly enjoy this street, head down left from the Coliseum Cafe along the sidewalk. The first shop you come to is a large bookshop, **Minerva Bookstore**, that specialises in Islamic literature. If that does not fuel your interest, in the next block to the right of Minerva, is the **Central Shoe Store**, that must rate as one of the largest shoe stores around. Further down, on the same side of the road as the Coliseum Cafe, there are a whole lot of older establishments that sell lampshades, pens and textiles.

Keep walking and about 600 metres (2,000 ft) from Minerva Bookstore, you will come to the junction of Jalan Tuanku Abdul Rahman and **Jalan Dang Wangi**. Cross the street at this junction and backtrack along the opposite side.

Among the first few shops worth visiting here are **Selangor Pewter** at No. 231 Jalan Tuanku Abdul Rahman, which has on display an exciting array of pewterware, a home-grown handicraft and **Peiping**

One-stop shopping – Globe Silk Store

Lace (two stores) at Nos. 223 and 217 which sell antiques.

One of the country's oldest department stores, **Globe Silk Store**, located further down, offers some of the cheapest clothing buys in the city. Globe prides itself on its low prices and high quality, a tradition it has maintained for almost 60 years. There are four floors of clothing, textiles, cosmetics and carpets in the Globe, while the top floor has a very presentable cafeteria-type restaurant. You may want to take a break with a cold drink and curry puff (pastry stuffed with curried vegetables and meat) here.

Another 150 to 200 metres (490 to 700 feet) further down from Globe, is **Chotimall**, another department store of repute. However, while Globe is egalitarian, Chotimall prides itself on being upmarket. Designer labels are the norm here, with a price structure to match. From Chotimall, walk down another 150 to 200 metres and you will come to another department store called **Mun Loong**. Here too, clothing bargains may be picked up, especially if a sale is on.

Further down from Mun Loong, the shops become more predictable, selling mainly clothing. There are a few shops that also sell costume jewellery, hair bands and other accessories. The prices

vary according to the material and workmanship involved, but be prepared to bargain. On Saturday evenings, the street is turned into a pedestrian mall and a night market sprouts up along the entire stretch. Like all night markets in Malaysia, the prices

Fabrics of all colours and designs

are cheap and the variety is staggering. Vendors sell everything, from fresh meat and vegetables to clothes and household items. Try not to miss this night bazaar – the atmosphere alone is worth experiencing.

As you continue down the street, you will first meet the junction with **Jalan Melayu** (Malay Street), then the massive intersection with **Jalan Tun Perak**. Turn left into Jalan Tun Perak. The Moorish building across the road was built during the colonial days to house the Information Department. It has since been renovated to accommodate the High Court.

As you walk down Jalan Tun Perak, you will pass the **United Asian Bank** building and a host of shops on the left, before coming to Jalan Melayu just before the bridge (opposite **Batek Malaysia**). Turn into Jalan Melayu. Across the road, the Klang River flows languidly, witness to the metamorphosis of a swamp to a sprawl. On your left are a row of shops that specialise in Indian fabrics,

particularly *saris*. Immediately after these shops is a speciality restaurant serving Punjabi food, called **Jaihind**, just after the Nova Scotia Bank. By this time, the afternoon heat would have begun to get to you, so stop over at the restaurant for a cold drink of *lassi*, which is made of Indian yogurt, and a confection called *jelabi* which looks like an orange-red pretzel.

A short distance up the road, turn right into **Jalan Masjid India**, an area of marked Indian-Muslim accent. Every available space on Jalan Masjid India, which runs parallel to Jalan Tuanku Abdul Rahman, is taken up by shops, restaurants and sidewalk stalls in a motley blend. Among them are artists, buskers and the veritable medicine seller stationed at corners with his concoctions – that allegedly cure

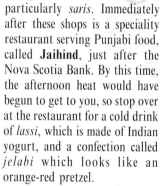

Bumper to bumper along Jalan Tuanku Abdul Rahman

any ailment from snake bites to sexual maladies – displayed on the pavement. For theatre appeal, it is hard to beat this genre of peddlers, a sure crowd puller with their fast-paced, excited narration of unbelievable medicinal wonders.

Jalan Masjid India begins ironically, with a cluster of Malay shops (Wisma Yakin) on your right. The shops sell clothes and food, but one of the more interesting ones specialises in *Jamu*, a traditional medicine of multiple properties.

Further down on the left is the Indian Muslim mosque after which the street is named. The mosque is not open to the public, but you can stop here a while to appreciate its architecture, which is quintessentially Indian Muslim. Notice the tall spires reminiscent of Taj Mahal-type structures.

Immediately left of the mosque, you will see a stretch of shops housed within the **Malayan Mansion**. Rising grey and grimy for

seven storeys, the mansion is one of the oldest buildings in this area. The first two levels are crammed with establishments that trade, wholesale or retail an enormous variety of merchandise. Diagonally opposite this is a similar block, called **Selangor Mansion**, that is similarly

Medicine man and his wares at Jalan Masjid India jammed. Almost anything can be bought in the two mansions, but the area is better known for its speciality shops dealing in Indian textiles, Indian ethnic music, brassware and other unusual items.

As you amble down the road, buy a drink of *mata kuching* (longan tea) or coconut water from one of the many drink vendors around. They are great cooling drinks and will help you keep your shirt on

Solemnity lines the face before prayer

A cosy niche in 'Little India'

in the sizzling heat. Along the way too, you can find public toilets indicated by the *Tandas* signs. Incidentally, the road branches into a fork in front of Selangor Mansion. The narrower street on the right is **Medan Bunus**. The broad divider explodes in a blaze of colour with buckets of freshly-cut blooms and gaudy garlands hanging in odd-looking wire netting enclosures. The flower-sellers here will thread the blossoms any way you want, from simple hair adornments to lavish bridal car arrangements.

Back onto Masjid India, the shops continue down the street. The buildings are of more recent vintage and the surroundings are cleaner. On your left is **Car and Company**, one of the country's oldest and best known sporting goods establishments. To the right of it is **Chamtan Hotel**, a budget lodging house that is a darling among out-of-city shoppers. Right at the end of the street are more shops, including money changers, a pharmacy and clothing stores.

Indian cutlery stores along this row specialise in Indian stainless steel cutlery. For some unfathomable reason, Indians like to eat off metal and not china, possiby because of a morbid fear of clumsy dishwashers. This habit is however far less prevalent among second and third generation Malaysian Indians.

Masjid India terminates in an unremarkable shopping mall called **Semua House**. There are a few shops here that sell costume jewellery, clothes, video cassettes and other similar merchandise but nothing you would not have already encountered. Semua House's main attraction lies in its air conditioning and the vending machine that dispenses canned or packet drinks. That may seem trite to you if you are reading this before venturing forth in Kuala Lumpur's afternoon heat. But after this walk, you will enter Semua House with the joy of an ant that has just discovered a sugar warehouse.

Traditional costume jewellery – Indian plastic bracelets

When you are through wandering around Semua House, backtrack along Jalan Masjid India and Jalan Melayu to Jalan Tun Perak and cross the bridge. Continue past the first intersection and turn left at the next traffic lights into **Lebuh Ampang**. This area is known as Little India, a throw-back to the time when the area was dominated by Indian shops. Today it is far more cosmopolitan but the name Little India has stuck nevertheless. There is a jewellery shop called **Batu Pahat Jeweller**, which deals in Indian-style fine filigree gold jewellery; a couple of old-time Chettiar money-lenders; *sari* shops and Indian restaurants.

At Little India, getting a taxi is seldom a problem. It is almost time for dinner, so from here, hail a cab and tell the driver to take you to the **Omar Khayyam Restaurant** on **Jalan Medan Tuanku**, on the upper end of Jalan Tuanku Abdul Rahman. To vary the flavour of the afternoon, have a North Indian dinner at Omar Khayyam. Try the *tandoori*, *kebab* and *lassi* (sweetened or salted diluted yogurt). A meal of *tandoori* and *kebab* costs about M$30.

3. Down The Valley

Train ride down the Klang Valley; sightseeing in Klang and suburbs; seafood dinner in the port.

This tour takes you down the **Klang Valley**, which lies roughly parallel to the historic boat trip 57 tin miners took 130 years ago, in search of tin and ended up founding Malaysia's capital city, Kuala Lumpur. The dense fetid jungle has all but disappeared however, under the onslaught of urbanisation. The Klang Valley is today the country's fastest growing, richest and most industrialised region.

The intriguing part of this tour is that it is done by train. Kuala

All's quiet at Klang Railway Station

Railbus to Klang

Lumpur's first link with the outside world was via a railway line built by Sir Frank Swettenham in 1886. Before its existence, travel to Kuala Lumpur was a malarial agony. In the words of Sir Frank Swettenham: "Over the roots, through the thorns, wading and swimming rivers and streams, ploughing through miles of bog and mud in the heat and the rain, stung by everything that stings (their name is legion) and usually spending two or three nights in the jungle with any kind of shelter that a chopper and the forest could supply."

The present Kuala Lumpur-Klang railway line remains faithful to the original route laid down by Swettenham over a century ago. For the most part, it follows the Klang River, which is now reduced to a silty polluted river.

Start this tour by having an early lunch of *yong tau foo* (stuffed tofu and vegetables) at a stall in an old sector of K.L. called **Brickfields**. Taxis from the city will take you there. You should try and finish lunch by 12.30 p.m. and then head for the railway station to board the 1.15 p.m. railbus to Klang.

The *yong tau foo* stall – with the signboard *Yong Tauhu* – is located along **Jalan Thambapillai** at the T-junction of **Jalan Tun Sambanthan 5**. It is a modest stall stashed between two fruit vendors, but clean and popular in the neighbourhood for its piping hot *yong tau foo* and *chee cheong fun* (rice flour rolls eaten with prawn paste). Pick from an array of fish balls, *tau foo* (bean curd), brinjal, chilli and other vegetables stuffed with minced pork or fish meat.

KTM

You can either choose to have your *yong tau foo* with or without broth. Chilli and sweet sauce are used as dips. For drinks: the drink stall in the same location which sells sugar cane juice and coconut water (with the soft pulp). A lunch like that should cost under M$4.

After lunch, hail a taxi to the railway station. The cab fare should be around M$3. At the station, go to any of the ticket booths and buy a one-way railbus ticket for the 1.15 p.m. train to Klang. The fare is M$1.40 for the one-hour train journey.

The first area the rail bus passes is the massive railroad yard at Brickfields, only a stone's throw from the place where you lunched. Brickfields is so named because of the numerous brick factories that were established around 1884 to fuel Swettenham's ambitious urban renewal plans. The factories could not meet the demand – one of the factors which stymied Swettenham's efforts – and today, not one of these remain.

Past Brickfields, the railbus picks up speed, passing the congested

Jalan Bangsar on the right, then swings past the massive studios of **Radio Televisyen Malaysia**, the state-owned broadcasting corporation. Called Angkasapuri, the complex also houses a regional training centre, the **Tun Abdul Razak Broadcasting Institute**. Past Angkasapuri, you will come to a green belt area called **Bukit Gasing**, that remains the last vestige of nature between the urban sprawl of Kuala Lumpur and its satellite district, **Petaling Jaya**.

Petaling Jaya, or P.J. as it is known among acronym-obsessed Malaysians, looms up ahead shortly. P.J. was developed as a low-cost housing scheme only in the late 1950s. Indeed, the railway traverses much of old P.J. Since then, the district has grown into the country's richest residential town, a middle-class mecca of over 500,000 inhabitants and its premiere industrial area. The statistics speak for themselves: the country's highest household incomes; the highest personal car ownership in Southeast Asia; the highest VCR ownership pattern in the region and so on.

During its journey through P.J., the railbus passes through slums and illegal squatter settlements. Like most rapidly growing towns, P.J. has had to contend with floods of rural emigrants who supply most of the menial workforce. Unable to share the wealth that brought them in the first place, they are forced to settle for a shanty-town life along the railway line.

The railbus takes you past **Sungai Way**, a suburb of P.J. (when a satellite town begins to have its own suburb, you know it has really arrived) where most of the electronics factories are located. On your left would be the giant **Guinness brewery**, one of the largest stout breweries outside Ireland, and **Kontena Nasional's** inland container depot, while on the right is the **Matsushita** air-conditioning factory, the largest of its kind in the world. Incidentally, Malaysia is one of the world's largest exporters of air-conditioners.

Past Sungai Way are several undeveloped tin mining areas,

Stately gardens lead to the Sultan Sulaiman Mosque

constant reminders of the impetus that brought development to the Klang valley in the first place. P.J. ends with its newest housing sub-division, **Subang Jaya**. There is a small station on the left and right behind it, a huge shopping mall, **Subang Parade**, touted as Asia's longest.

Even religious detail is firmly atop the mosque's gate

After Subang Jaya, the railbus enters another green belt albeit briefly, then into another massive development, **Shah Alam**. The new capital of the State of Selangor, Shah Alam is another successful residential town, developed from only the 1970s. The line traverses the industrial part of the town, already larger than that of P.J.'s and still growing.

On your left would be the **High Technology Industrial Park** and right behind, though not visible from the train, is the **Perusahaan Otomobil Nasional (Proton)** factory, manufacturers of Malaysia's national car, the **Proton Saga**. Further down, on the right, is the towering spire and powder blue dome of **Sultan Salahuddin Abdul Aziz Shah Mosque**. The mosque is the largest in Malaysia, and reflects a blend of traditional Islamic as well as local Malay architecture. The dome is believed to be one of the largest of its kind in

the world, measuring 57 metres (187 ft) in diameter and 60 metres (197 ft) high. The four minarets, nine metres (29½ ft) in diameter and 153 metres (505 ft) high, are the tallest in the world.

Next to the mosque, the skyline is dominated by the office towers of downtown Shah Alam. Further down the line, you will see the towering sprawl of the **Mara Institute of Technology**, the country's largest polytechnic, before passing the **Connaught Bridge power station**, which marks the end of the city.

While there is little semblance of a green belt between Shah Alam and Klang, the distinction between the two towns is instantly visible. Klang is old, in fact, older than Kuala Lumpur. The streets pull away from the railway line haphazardly, a legacy of a time when the railroad was the only link between a whole lot of otherwise isolated communities. The streets languidly meander between shops, houses and overgrown rain trees.

About 10 km (6.2 miles) to the west is **Port Klang**, Malaysia's biggest and busiest port, but the town after which it is named seems totally unaffected. In contrast, **Klang's** railway station is small but quaint. There is a small shop selling soft drinks and snacks such as potato crisps and popcorn, and you may want to use the reasonably clean rest rooms here. Once outside the station, you will see the taxi stand. If you are doing this tour on a weekend, please note that taxis at the station are scarce. In that case, just walk along the road facing the station's main entrance, which is called **Jalan Stesen**, till you come to the post office on your left. There are usually taxis waiting at this spot.

There are no tour bus facilities in Klang, so you would have to make do with hiring a taxi for the trip. The rate would vary according to the time the taxi is hired, but would be in the region of M$15 per hour. It is advisable to agree upon the hire rate before boarding the taxi.

The one-time capital of Selangor, Klang is now completely overshadowed by Shah Alam. However, it has a long and proud history that has left its mark on the town. Tell the taxi driver to take you around the town centre. Klang never went through the rash of urban renewal that K.L. did, where lovely old homes and shophouses were torn down and replaced with glass-and-steel cuboids. Much of Klang town still retains a lot of its old character. In fact, many of its buildings have been around even before World War II. This makes it an excellent place for a historical monuments tour. Start your tour by telling the taxi driver to take you to the **Kota Raja Mahadi** on **Jalan Kota**. This is a fort built by one of the main protagonists in the Selangor Civil War of 1867. Across the town along **Jalan Tepi Sungai**, is **Gedung Raja Abdullah**, which was built in 1856 by Raja Mahadi's opponent, Raja Abdullah. The building now houses the **Selangor State Museum** and is well worth visiting, not just for the many exhibits on the history of the state, but by virtue of its distinctive architecture as well.

On **Jalan Timor** is the **Sultan Sulaiman Mosque**, built by the British in the 19th century and given to Sultan Sulaiman. It has an interesting blend of British Imperial, Moorish and Arabic architectural styles. A British architect designed the mosque. Admission is free to all the three places mentioned above.

Another building that features a similar architectural confusion as the Masjid Sultan Sulaiman is the **Istana Alam Shah**, the palace of the Sultan of Selangor, located on **Jalan Istana**. The Sultan no longer resides here but in Shah Alam. This palace is today maintained for official functions. It is not open to the public, but there is a specially built concrete bunker about 100 metres (330 ft) to the left (as you face the main gate) from which you can enjoy a panoramic view of the palace and its grounds.

The above tour sequence takes you from one side of Klang town to the other.

After you have finished touring Klang town, it should be close to late evening. If you wish to catch the train back to K.L., note that the last train for the city leaves Klang at 7.19 p.m. However, taxis that ply the Klang-K.L. route are easily available. Skip the train and have a sumptuous seafood meal at Klang port. Tell your taxi driver to take you to the **Port View Restaurant** along **Jalan Wharf** in the port. This is an old and popular seafood restaurant overlooking the sea, where you can relax with a pre-dinner drink while dinner is being prepared. The food here is cooked mostly Chinese and Western style. Try the steamed prawns or chilli crabs, or get the waiter to recommend the catch of the day.

Relax over dinner and when you have finished, hail another cab to the K.L. taxi stand from which you can catch taxis that ply into the city. The fare to K.L. is M$24 and the journey should take about an hour. On the way into K.L. you will have a chance to get a closer look at Shah Alam and Petaling Jaya. Swettenham would never have believed it.

A stately mansion: Istana Alam Shah

Day TRIPS

Each of the following tours will take you from morning to early evening or later to complete. They are designed to give you a comprehensive feel of rural Malaysia with some typical K.L. attractions. From the mundane of touristic playgrounds at Genting Highlands, to the very unusual – Pulau Ketam's stilted community – the tours promise pure enjoyment at relatively little expense. Aside from touristic Genting Highlands, the other places recommended below are relatively away from the beaten track and hence retain a quaint, unpretentious air. They are mainly patronised by the locals, therefore the trips also give an honest insight into Malaysian society.

1. Genting Highlands

Full day

Kuala Lumpur's prime hangout for the rich, **Genting Highlands,** boasts of the country's largest theatre restaurant and its only casino. The masses throng the place too. After all, there is a 21-hole golf course, Swiss-style cable car complex, amusement park and boating lake. Located about 2,000 metres (6,500 ft) above sea level, the midday temperature at Genting Highlands is only about 24 to 25°C (75 to 76°F), a respite from the city's sweltering heat.

Rolling hills to Genting Highlands

Hotel and amusement park

Scheduled air-conditioned bus services serve the resort and can be boarded at the Tun Razak Bus Station. They run every hour on the hour, from 7 a.m. to 7 p.m. The fare is about M$10 one way. Taxis can also be availed at the same terminal for about M$21 for a one-way journey. Another option is the hourly air-conditioned bus service from the Puduraya Bus Terminal which plies the same route and costs M$4.50, inclusive of the cable car ride. The last bus leaves at 7 p.m.

A convenient way of savouring Genting Highland's delights would be to take the bus or taxi up to the **Awana Country and Golf Club**. Stop here and enjoy the splendid scenery. Then take the cable car that operates from the building right opposite Awana's main gate. The cable car ride, at M$2.50 per person one-way, takes you to the main Genting Highlands complex. Cable car services begin daily at 8 a.m. and run once every 45 minutes.

At Genting Highlands, there is little chance of losing your way around. Clear directions to the prime spots of amusement and entertainment are indicated by signboards bearing directional arrows. If you wish to enter the casino, bear in mind you will have to produce your passport.

The amusement park consists of the usual fare of merry-go-rounds and ferris wheels. Rides cost between M$1 and M$2 each. A Disney-type theme park is under construction however, and promises attractions a lot less mundane when completed in 1993. If you are a golf enthusiast you might like to know that green fees are M$40 to M$80. For meals, either eat at any of the hotel restaurants, which offer both local and western fare, or at the coffee-shop restaurant located near the amusement park area.

The last bus leaves Genting Highlands at 6 p.m., while the last cable car departs at 5 p.m.

2. Lentang Recreational Forest

Full day

For rain forest buffs, the **Lentang Recreational Forest**, 52 km (32.3 miles) from K.L., offers many hours of browsing. There is a pristine stream that runs through the forest, complete with waterfall and a short run of rapids. Swimming is possible in some stretches. While the forest has been substantially disturbed around the stream, mainly for the construction of tourist facilities – picnic areas, toilets, bathing rooms and shelters – numerous hiking trails will take you into unspoilt virgin jungle.

JABATAN HUTAN NEGERI PAHANG DARUL MAKMUR

Lentang is reached by taking the bus to **Bentong** from the **Tun Razak Bus Station**. The service is operated by the Central Pahang Omnibus Company and costs about M$2.50 one way. The bus journey would take roughly an hour. Be sure to tell the conductor to warn you when to get off – the Lentang Recreational Forest is just before Bentong and the bus would stop there first. A taxi service to Bentong is also available. Fares would be in the region of M$3 one way.

If you are planning an extensive hike through the jungle, consult the Forest Rangers who are on duty at the site. There is little chance of being attacked by large wildlife, but there are snakes, giant centipedes and scorpions around. Another real risk is getting lost in the myriad of *rintis* (tracks) that weave through the jungle. Although the hiking trails are marked to some extent, parts of these may be obscured. The Forest Rangers would be able to give relevant information on trails to follow and more importantly, keep a look out if you do not return on time. Of course, the time of your hike really depends on how far you want to go, but we advise that you should not be too ambitious.

Please note there are no restaurants of any worth in Lentang. There is a small food stall at the entrance which serves cold drinks and Malay ethnic food, but if that is not for you, consider buying food and drinks at the bus station.

A slice of nature – the Lentang Recreational Forest

Man-made luxury amidst nature's wonders

3. Mimaland

Half day

Short for "Malaysia-in-Miniature", **Mimaland**, located 15 km (9.3 miles) east of K.L. along the old K.L.-Bentong Road, does not quite live up to its name. Nonetheless, it does make for a quiet, pleasant, morning of fishing, tennis, jogging or squash. Being reasonably close to the city, most city taxis will take you there, the fare is about M$10 to M$15. Return services may not be so regular, so it may be prudent for you to negotiate with the taxi driver to pick you up from Mimaland afterwards. Entrance fees to Mimaland are M$2 per adult and M$1 per child under 12 years.

Bring your own line and tackle if you plan to fish; pack a bath towel if you plan to swim. Swimmers may be interested in what has been described as South-east Asia's longest stream-fed swimming pool. Admission to the swimming pool costs M$2 on weekdays and M$3 on weekends. The changing rooms at the pool complex do not provide towels.

Both tennis and squash courts are quite easily available and per hour rentals on weekdays are M$4 and on weekends, M$6. Courts are available from 10 a.m. to 10 p.m. There is a substantial boating lake where rides on rowboats, aqua bikes and canoes are available. Hourly rental rates are M$2.50 for rowboats, M$5 for aqua bikes and M$3 for canoes. For children, there is an extensively-landscaped playground with the usual swings and slides. There is also a life-sized fibreglass dinosaur display (no charges to gawk at this).

The **Pelanduk Restaurant**, next to the reception counter in the main complex, serves local and western food. At the swimming pool, there is the **Pelitas**, which serves fast food and snacks such as sandwiches, burgers and fried rice.

4. Pulau Ketam

Full day

A day trip with a difference, **Pulau Ketam** (Crab Island) is located about 1½-hour's boat ride from **Port Klang**. Its intrepid pioneers discovered it about a century ago to be nothing more than a mangrove mudpile that almost disappeared during high tide. Instead of looking for greener pastures, they stayed put, building their houses on stilts. Today, a whole township, complete with side-

walks, grocers, power station, telephone exchange and girlie bars, all on stilts, have erupted on the island. The main occupation is fishing and besides the quaint scenery, the town's restaurants serve the freshest seafood around. You might like to check out the **Nam Hong** or **Kim Hor** restaurants, both of which dish up the speciality, "steamed *sembilang*" or catfish. Some city folk come all the way to Pulau Ketam to buy fresh seafood from the villagers.

Away from the mayhem of city life

To get there, take a taxi from the **Klang Bus Station** in **Jalan Bandar** to the public jetty at **Port Klang** – the fare should be around M$6. Scheduled ferry services to the island start at 8 a.m. and operate every two hours. The fare is M$2 one way per person. The last ferry leaves the island at 5 p.m., an important consideration in light of the fact that no rental accommodation on the island is available.

Stilt houses adorn the island's banks

As Pulau Ketam was never built for tourism, this is the perfect place to soak in the atmosphere of an unfabricated, unspoilt fishing village. Except for a little stroll around the small island to look at the village on stilts and a meal at the seafood restaurants, there are no other tourist trappings to keep you amused. Two or three hours here would be more than sufficient and will leave you relaxed and totally satisfied at having discovered a relatively uncommercial spot near Kuala Lumpur.

5. Morib

Half day

If you had a chance to peruse all the tourist literature published on Malaysia, you would have noticed that pictures of pristine sandy beaches lined with swaying palms often emblazon the front or back covers and the centrepiece of these glossy brochures. In fact, this whole tropical beach bit is a major selling point in the Malaysian tourist industry although much of it is an oversell.

But K.L. is not totally devoid of the sun and sea accolades which Penang or Kuantan boast of, although its assets of such sort tend to be more modest. The nearest beach resort to K.L. is **Morib**, a small stretch of sand about 76 km (47.2 miles) west of Kuala Lumpur. It is fringed by a small township and a nine-hole golf course at the **Sri Morib Golf Club**, which is one of the most picturesque in the country.

Soaking in the sun

To get to Morib, take a taxi from the **Klang Bus Station** in **Jalan Bandar.** The fare is about M$50 for a whole taxi or about M$12 per passenger if it carries a full complement of four passengers. There are also direct bus services to Morib via Banting. The buses leave the Klang Bus Station at 9 and 11 a.m. and the fare is M$2.

Start the day with breakfast at **Sri Devi Restaurant**, an Indian ethnic establishment located at 45, Jalan Travers. Breakfast should consist of *thosai,* a rice-flour-based pancake cooked in ghee and served with lentils; coconut chutney and fish curry. From Sri Devi, the bus station is only about a M$3 taxi ride away.

The drive to Morib (it takes about an hour) can be as entertaining as the resort itself. A significant portion of the road traverses oil palm country. Kilometre after kilometre, oil palm trees stretch out in neat rows, underscoring Malaysia's position as the world's largest exporter of palm oil.

Sri Morib Golf Club

There are few amenities at Morib, so for the most part, you must come armed with towels, sun-tan lotion, bathing cap and beach mat. To avoid the crowd, go there on a weekday. If golfing interests you, contact the **Sri Morib Golf Club** (Tel: 867-1732) in advance to ascertain availability of greens. Green fees are about M$15 per day. An advantage of this arrangement is that after the golf game, you can spend the rest of the day at the beach, since it just fringes the course, and use the club's facilities such as the restroom and showers.

If golfing is not your cup of tea, rent a room at the **Sri Morib Hotel**, located at the 28½ milestone along the Klang-Morib road. Your taxi driver should know where it is. Day rates are about M$20 to M$36, depending on the size of the room taken. It is a medium class hotel, but offers the convenience of rest rooms, showers and the possibility of an afternoon nap as well.

Both the rest house and the Sri Morib Golf Club have restaurants serving local and western cuisine, seafood being the most popular.

6. Kuala Selangor

Half day

Standing at the estuary of the Selangor River, **Kuala Selangor** once played capital to the Sultanate of Selangor. In those times, the river was a vital means of communication to the otherwise impenetrable interior. Anyone who controlled the river controlled the hinterland as well. The state of Selangor, in this respect, had three great river systems – the Langat, Klang and Selangor – and the respective nobilities that controlled them constantly bickered for dominance. Ultimately, the Klang won and the valley it has scoured is the nation's fastest growing urban area. Both the Kuala Langat (located at the estuary of the Langat) and Kuala Selangor slipped into obscurity.

However, the greatness the town once knew remains in the form of ruined fortresses, lighthouses and a mausoleum. Have your breakfast at the hotel, then make a beeline for **Klang Bus Station** at **Jalan Bandar** to catch a taxi to Kuala Selangor. The fare should

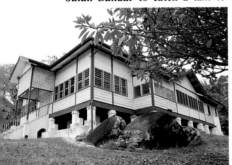

be about M$45 for the hour-long journey. Tell the taxi driver to drop you at the resthouse. Some tourists get their taxi driver to stay on for the day for the latter can sometimes double up as a guide and also solves the

Colonial elegance – Bukit Melawati Resthouse

problem of the ride back to the city. Do however remember to settle on a fee before you embark on your excursion. The **Kuala Selangor resthouse** is a quaint colonial structure on Bukit Melawati, the highest point in the town. Have a drink or refresh yourself inside.

Back to nature – chalets in the park

There are two forts that were built to defend the town. The larger and the only one open to the public, is **Kota Melawati** (formerly Fort Atingsburg), which stands on Bukit Melawati. It is 100 metres (330 ft) diagonally opposite the resthouse, although dense vegetation obscures the view of the fort from the rest house. The fort has not been used for close to a century and it is extensively landscaped. It provides a breathtaking view of the Straits of Malacca and the lowlands of the Selangor valley.

Standing tall – the Atingsburg Lighthouse

From the fort, you can easily walk to other places of interest in the immediate vicinity. Signboards along the meandering pathways provide excellent guidance and there is little chance of losing your way. Some of the places you should visit at Bukit Melawati include the **Atingsburg Lighthouse**, which is still functional; the **Royal Mausoleum**, which enshrines the remains of Selangor's ancient Bugis kings; and a tradititonal cultural stage. There is also a museum which has displays of artifacts from the town's heyday but it is closed for renovations. Check with the Tourist Information counters for opening times.

Lunch should be taken at the resthouse, since it is not only convenient, but affords a view of the town and sea that is hard to find elsewhere. The restaurant serves local and some Continental cuisine, but the fried rice is recommended.

After lunch, backtrack to the visitor's centre and take the steep flight of stairs just outside to the **Kuala Selangor Nature Park**. The park consists of 250 hectares (618 acres) of swamp and is a sanctuary for about 130 species of birds. It is said that some 100,000 wading birds pass through on their annual migration. Man-made lakes have been created and for bird watchers, there are observation hideouts.

Taxis for the return journey are available outside the resthouse. If you would like to spend more time here, the nature park offers chalets for overnight stays.

Next to the racy attractions of Manila and Bangkok, Kuala Lumpur might come across like a bastion of Victorian morality. The naughty stuff is there of course, but it is underground and illicit. The sexual profligacy that have made some Asian capitals enticements for the male libido is absent here.

This does not mean that one's evening must be spent in a hotel room. In one respect, K.L.'s nightlife does stand out – variety. Whether it is shopping, night clubbing, disco or pub crawling, there is a broad spread of night time activity that many find engrossing.

1. Night Markets

Every day of the week, the city authorities close off a street or two to vehicular traffic, and then proceed to turn it over to small-time traders and hawkers. The *pasar malam*, or night markets, are a hallowed institution in Malaysia, bazaars of exuberance and colour. The petty traders that service the night markets range from vendors of fresh vegetables, meat and fish, food, to tools, electronics, music cassette tapes, flowers, fruits....

It is not just the variety of merchandise that makes the night markets special, however. The markets are social institutions as well, providing the opportunity for neighbours and friends to meet in the cool of the evening.

Strains that still endear, the Chinese opera

Since night markets are mobile, you will have to check out their location on a given day. Normally, this information can be obtained at **City Hall**, Kuala Lumpur or at most Tourist Information Centres.

Some popular night market sites are: **Jalan Angsana**, off Jalan Tun Sambanthan on Wednesday. **Kampung Datuk Keramat** and in **Damansara Utama, Petaling Jaya** on Friday. **Jalan Tuanku Abdul Rahman** and in **Bangsar** on Saturday. **Taman Tun Dr Ismail** on Sunday.

Bargains at Chow Kit Bazaar

2. Night Clubbing

Night clubs are found in most major hotels in the city, though there are a number of independent operators as well. Night clubs are popular mainly among Chinese businessmen for the decor and ambience: *papier mâché* dragons, raucous businessmen indulging in cocktails like brandy and coke, and Taiwanese crooners belting out Cantonese pop songs. Hotel night clubs are usually more cosmopolitan. Among the better clubs in K.L. are the **Shangri-La** at Puduraya, Jalan Pudu; **Pertama** at the Pertama Shopping Complex, Jalan Tuanku Abdul Rahman; **Campbell** at Campbell Shopping Centre, Jalan Dang Wangi; **Flory** at K.L. Plaza, Jalan Bukit Bintang; and **Grosder** at the Federal Hotel, Jalan Bukit Bintang.

3. Discos

K.L.'s real strength in night-time entertainment are discos. There are a profusion of these in the city, some very good, many mediocre, but all worth patronising. All good hotels have discos as standard fixtures. Discos operate on weekdays, from 9 p.m. to 1 a.m.; on weekends, till 2 a.m.

Rumours features in K.L. Merlin; **Club Oz** in the Shangri-La; and **Tin Mine** in K.L. Hilton, among others. Independents include **The Turf** at 10 Jalan Kia Peng; **Seventh Avenue** in Menara Apera ULG in Jalan Raja Chulan; **Hippodrome Worldwide** at the Ampang Park Shopping Complex; **Limelight** at 3 Cangkat Raja Chulan; **Stargazer** at the Semua House, Medan Bunus; **Faces** at Jalan Ampang and **Sapphire** in Yow Chuan Plaza at Jalan Tun Razak.

The list is by no means exhaustive and you should enquire from the tourist information services for further details on the matter. A good source is the *Malay Mail* newspaper, an afternoon tabloid that gives a comprehensive listing of entertainment spots around the city and a run down on their entertainment value.

4. Pubs

One of the more endearing traditions left behind by the British colonialists is the pub. Modelled after the public drinking houses found in Britain, pubs play a similar role in Malaysian society. Office workers, businessmen and executives congregate in these watering holes after work to wash down their tribulations with a pint or two of beer before trudging home.

Malaysian pubs are different from their British counterparts with respect to a couple of points. Firstly, almost all serve a sizeable range of food – the pub fare of sandwiches, burgers and French fries – though you would be hard put to find pub grub of any quality. Secondly, many pubs feature live music and almost all have oversized sound systems, though some only play "muzak".

Among the better pubs around would be **The Pub** in Shangri-La Hotel; **Dinty's** along Jalan Tun Sambanthan; **Castell** in Jalan Bukit Bintang; **All That Jazz** along Jalan 19/36, Petaling Jaya; **New Copper Grill** in Menara Promet, Jalan Sultan Ismail; and **Ceejay's** off Jalan P. Ramlee.

5. Karaoke Lounges

While this is a comparatively new development in the local entertainment scene, it has caught on fast. Karaoke lounges are essentially spruced up bars equipped with audio facilities that filter out the lyrics from recorded pop music, leaving behind only the instrumental background. This is to allow their customers to indulge in their childhood ambition of becoming musicians or singers.

K.L.'s suburbs are peppered with karaoke lounges serving a mainly blue-collared crowd. There are quite a few however, that cater to executives, particularly Japanese expatriates. Such lounges come with "guest relations officers", pretty faces that offer conversation, join you in a drink and laugh at your jokes. Overt hanky-panky is disallowed (but as the management generally puts it, what the guest relations officer does after working hours is none of their business).

The better karaoke lounges would include **Club Fukiko** in Menara Promet, Jalan Sultan Ismail; **Lai-Lai Karaoke Lounge** in the Sungai Wang Plaza; **Ono Supper Club** at Wisma Selangor Dredging, Jalan Ampang; and **Tapagayo** at Jalan Bukit Bintang. Hours: weekdays 9 p.m. - 1 a.m.; weekends till 2 a.m.

6. Music

One would have thought that with as musically inclined a society as Malaysia's, finding good live stuff would be no problem. However, Malaysians prefer to listen to their favourites in the comfort of an easy chair, getting their kicks from the hi-fi, radio or TV.

Still, there are a few night spots in Kuala Lumpur which offer live music. Those who are into jazz would want to visit **All That Jazz**, 14 Jalan 19/36, Petaling Jaya, or **Riverbank** in the Central Market in the heart of Kuala Lumpur.

Country 'n' Western fans would appreciate the **Longhorn Pub** in Damansara Utama, Petaling Jaya.

There are also places with nostalgic music as their theme. **Blue Moon** in Equatorial Hotel plays oldies from the 1950s, while **Betelnut** along Jalan Ipoh spins 1960s and 1970s favourites.

7. Cultural Performances

These are held in K.L. quite regularly, some of them in the open air. On Saturday nights, shows by local entertainers are held at the **City Hall Auditorium** from 8.30 p.m. You can obtain free admission passes at the City Hall's information counter. Saturday night performances are also held at **Sulaiman Court**, next to Pertama Complex along Jalan Raja Laut.

Daily shows are held at the **Malaysia Tourist Information Complex** on Jalan Ampang. Cultural shows are performed at its mini-auditorium at 3.30 p.m., while audio-visual shows are screened at 10 a.m., 11 a.m., 2.45 p.m., and 5 p.m. Admission is free.

Central Market too has presentations of dance and drama at its riverside amphitheatre. These take place from Wednesday to Sunday, beginning from 7.45 p.m. Admission is free.

Details regarding these shows can be obtained from Tourist Information Centres, City Hall or Central Market.

Catch a cultural evening at Central Market

A Glutton's Paradise

Kuala Lumpur is probably not the most conducive place a dieter can come across. The variety of food is endless, the portions large and the prices reasonable. In the end, it is probably wiser to let your epicurean urges go wild and sample what the city has to offer.

You have a choice of Malay, Chinese, Indian, Portuguese, Nyonya, Continental, beside more exclusive French, Russian, Iranian, Italian, Japanese and Korean. Even the major cuisines have sub-types that are radically different. Indian food, for example, covers South Indian, Punjabi, Moghul and Indian Muslim.

If that does not boggle you, then perhaps the varied circumstances in which they are served might. There are restaurants with Maxim-type decor and a price list to match. There are middle class restaurants that are not so hefty on the pocket. Then there are the street vendors whose stalls erupt every evening, around every street corner, like mushrooms after a heavy rain. The quality of the food, however, has nothing to do with where they are served. Some of K.L.'s best come from hawkers who would not know how to spell Maxim's, yet cater to a clientele so exclusive, they qualify as the mould on the upper crust of Malaysian society.

The list below is not exhaustive, but a complete guide to gluttony in K.L. is a book in itself. Take a bit of each, be adventurous and start on that diet tomorrow.

All you ever need to quench your thirst

Chillies, for the spicy touch to your curry

Malay Food

With 13 states and culinary specialities within each region, the array of Malay food is almost infinite. Provincial cooking is differentiated largely by taste and flavour; northern cooking tends to be *pedas* (spicy hot) and sometimes sour, reflecting a Thai influence. Southern cuisine, on the other hand, is milder with a taste of Javanese. And in Negri Sembilan, under Minangkabau influence, chillies are used generously for an extra kick or burn, depending on how seasoned one's taste buds are.

The richness of Malay food comes from the use of coconut milk (*santan*) and spices, and its aroma and flavour from fragrant roots and grasses. Sweets are heavily laced with coconut milk and palm sugar, so go easy on them.

Yazmin Restaurant, 6 Jalan Kia Peng. Tel: 241-5655.
Both the buffet and menu offer a good variety of dishes from all over the country. There is an evening cultural performance.

Rasa Utara, Bukit Bintang Plaza, Jalan Bukit Bintang. Tel: 243-8243.
Specialises in northern Malay cuisine. Try the *ayam percik*, a hot, sour chicken dish that the state of Kelantan is proud of.

Satay Anika, Bukit Bintang Plaza, Jalan Bukit Bintang. Tel: 248-3113.
Specialises in *satay*, meat barbequed over burning charcoal. Choose

an assortment of chicken, beef or mutton *satay*, which should be eaten with a sweetish, hot peanut sauce and cubes of steamed rice called *ketupat*. Besides this restaurant, *satay* is sold in any of the ubiquitous hawker stalls around K.L.

Bunga Raya Restaurant, Level 2, Putra World Trade Centre. Tel: 293-3888.
A new restaurant with somewhat upmarket prices. Conveniently located, near the Chow Kit shopping area.

Nelayan Floating Restauran, Titiwangsa Lake Gardens. Tel: 422-8600.
A restaurant built on a floating platform in one of K.L.'s largest gardens. The accent is on seafood; the style of cooking is either Chinese or Malay. Try the steamed sea bass. There is also a nightly cultural performance while you dine.

Restoran Sri Pinang, Lower Ground Floor, Menara Aik Hua. Tel: 230-6170.
Variety of local favourites like *nasi kandar*, *mee rebus* and *murtabak*.

Mubarak Restoran, 1st floor, Stadium Merdeka, Jalan Stadium. Serves Indian-Muslim cuisine, famed for its fish-head curry, fried chicken and squid.

Chinese Food

Every provincial variety is available, be it Cantonese, Hokkien, Hakka, Teochew, Hainanese, Shanghainese, Peking, Taiwanese or Szechuan. Some of the cooking has become so localised they can only be labelled Malaysian, such as *bak-kut-teh*, pork stewed in a soup of five-spice powder and coriander; K.L. Hokkien mee, noodles stir fried with prawns and strips of pork in rich prawn based gravy;

Preserved duck eggs, an inexpensive delicacy

stir fried with prawns and strips of pork in rich prawn based gravy; and Ipoh *sah hor fun*, thick flat noodles cooked with meats.

Overseas Restaurant, ground floor, Central Market. No phone. Conveniently located at the Central Market mall, serves a whole gamut of Chinese food.

Restoran Sze Chuan, 42-3 Jalan Sultan Ismail. Tel: 248-2806. Szechuan cooking is unusual in that it is generally quite spicy, with chillies and pepper used quite liberally. Most meats are smoked. The squid fried in cashew nuts and chilli fried shrimps are especially recommended.

Teochew Restaurant, 272 Jalan Pudu. Tel: 241-6572.
Good *dim sum* – sweetmeats and savoury tidbits, steamed, fried, stewed or braised.

Hakka Restaurant, 231 Jalan Bukit Bintang. Tel: 985-8492.
Hakka food features lots of braised meat dishes.

Golden Phoenix Restaurant, Hotel Equatorial, Jalan Sultan Ismail. Tel: 261-7777.
Serves mainly Cantonese cuisine with specialities such as sizzling venison, braised abalone and salt-baked prawns.

Shang Palace, Shangri-La Hotel, Jalan Sultan Ismail. Tel: 232-2388. One of the best Chinese restaurants in the city.

Formosa Restaurant, 26 Jalan SS 2/67, Petaling Jaya. Tel: 776-1289. Serves Taiwanese food, known especially for steamboat – a do-it-yourself meal in which raw meats and greens are cooked in a boiling cauldron of rich soup stock.

Ipoh Chicken Restaurant, 107 Jalan Gasing, Petaling Jaya.
Tel: 756-0958. Popular for its chicken rice and king beansprouts.

Marco Polo Restaurant, 1st floor, Wisma Lim Foo Yong,, Jalan Raja Chulan. Tel: 242-5595.
Traditional Cantonese cuisine. Try the steamed fish or bamboo shoot

Esquire Kitchen, 1st floor, Sungai Wang Plaza, Jalan Sultan Ismail. Tel: 248-5006. Known for its Chinese dumplings, pork dishes and affordable prices.

Indian Food

While the curries of South India are chilli hot and have a coconut milk base, the cuisine of the north is bland in comparison and sometimes sweet. Yogurt is preferred over coconut milk and the taste is derived more from the spices used, and also tends to be drier.

A typical South Indian banana leaf meal is quite an enjoyable experience. For under M$5, you get to choose from a selection of hot curries, meats and vegetables. As an introduction to Indian food though, it might cost your digestive system some discomfort, especially as the "heat" of the meal is usually compounded by the poor air-conditioning (or total lack of it), that is characteristic of these restaurants. Still, if you are game, try any of the following places:

Krishna Curry House, 10 Jalan SS 51A/222, Petaling Jaya. Tel: 756-4920.
Highly rated. Try the mutton and mushrooms. Plus point: has air-conditioning on the first floor.

Sri Devi, Jalan Travers, Brickfields. Tel: 274-4173.
The spicy dry fried mutton is highly recommended.

Mathai, Restoran Lay Sin, 250, Jalan Tun Sambanthan (below Peking Hotel), Brickfields. No phone.
Best known for its fried fish.

Meal on banana leaf

Iskcon Govinda's Restaurant, 16-1, 1st floor, Jalan Bunus 6, Masjid India. Tel: 298-6785.
Serves three types of vegetarian set lunches daily.

Lotus Restaurant, 15, Jalan Gasing, Petaling Jaya. Tel: 792-8795.
Air-conditioned. The spread of sweetmeats is too tempting to resist.

North Indian restaurants offers a range of Moghul cuisine; from *tandoori*, *tikka* and *kebab* to *naan* and *paratha*. Chillies are added on request.

Bijian, Subang Parade, Subang Jaya. No phone.

Shiraz Restaurant, 1 Jalan Medan Tuanku. Tel: 291-0035.

Omar Khayyam Restaurant, 5 Jalan Medan Tuanku. Tel: 291-1016.

Devi Annapoorna Restaurant, 94 Jalan Maarof, Bangsar. Tel: 255-6443.
Serves vegetarian food.

Bilal Restaurant, 33 Jalan Ampang. Tel: 238-0804.

Kasibrahim Restaurant, Jalan Tun Sambanthan, Brickfields. No phone. Serves typical Punjabi cuisine.

Nyonya Food

A delicious hybrid of Chinese and Malay cuisines, Nyonya food has its own flavours: hot, sour and aromatic. The liberal use of coconut milk, spices, chillies, pungent roots and aromatic leaves, results in rich and often heavy dishes. Northern Nyonya food is Thai-influenced, evidenced in the unmistakable searing hot, sour taste while in the south, more Malay influences have crept into the sauces. Desserts and sweets are creamy and generously laced with coconut milk and sugar. Below are some restaurants you may want to check out:

Restoran Matic Sri Saloma, 109 Jalan Ampang, Malaysian Tourist Information Complex. Tel: 243-4817.
Serves both Nyonya and Malay specialities such as *otak-otak*, *fish head curry* and *kuih pye ti*.

Sri Melaka Restaurant, 7, Jalan 52/8, Merdeka Square, New Town Centre, Petaling Jaya. Tel: 756-3497.
Offers Thai dishes as well.

Dondang Sayang Restaurant, 28, Jalan Telawi 5, Bangsar. Tel: 254-9388.
Tasty dishes, but somewhat pricey.

Nyonya Restaurant, 52 Jalan SS2/24, Petaling Jaya. Tel: 775-9709. Specialities of the day are worth trying as they are set meals with a variety of Nyonya favourites.

Thai Food

Since local cuisine is, to some extent, influenced by Thai taste and cooking style, many of the restaurants specialising in northern cuisine offer Thai dishes too. Conversely, Thai restaurants that boast of authentic Thai cooking often have on their menus Nyonya, Chinese and Malay dishes.

Restaurant Seri Chiangmai, 14 Jalan Perak. Tel: 248-2927.

Chilli Padi Restaurant, 2nd floor, The Mall. Tel: 442-4319.

Thai Kitchen, 28 Jalan SS 2/61, Petaling Jaya. Tel: 774-6426.

Sri Thai Restaurant, Wisma Selangor, Jalan University, Petaling Jaya. Tel: 756-3535.

Sukothai Restaurant, Damansara Utama, Petaling Jaya. No phone.

Sri Siam Restaurant, 58 Jalan SS 2/24, Petaling Jaya. Tel: 775-3076.

Seafood

Seafood is another great Malaysian favourite and there are hundreds of ways fish, prawns, crabs, squid and shellfish are prepared. In Malay cooking, the seafood is hot and spicy; in Chinese, steamed and stir-fried; in Indian cooking, curried and fried. But whatever the cooking style, seafood restaurants are, thankfully, not confined to the coastal states. If seafood is your delight, you may want to try the outlets named here. Roadside stalls also dish up some of K.L.'s best seafood.

Eden Village, Jalan Raja Chulan. Tel 241-4027.
Eden Gardenia, Jalan SS22/23, Petaling Jaya.
Both are the latest to join a successful chain of restaurants which originated in Penang. They feature fresh airflown lobsters, oysters and salmon. The decor in both comes complete with coral lamps, wall murals depicting marine life and tanks of fish and prawns. Most of the food is cooked continental style, and both selection and prices are reasonable. The K.L. outlet has a nightly cultural show.

Subang View Seafood, 229, Airport Road. Tel: 746-1401.
Situated next to the Kuala Lumpur International Airport, this place has an all-timber decor, offers fast service and tasty food cooked in various Chinese styles, served to the sounds of planes landing and taking off.

Bright lights will beckon diners

Restoran Y.S., Airport Road, right next to Subang View Seafood. Tel: 746-1407.
Huge Sri Lankan crabs are the speciality – cooked in the style of your choice – at this unpretentious open-air restaurant.

New Nanking Seafood, 236 Airport Road. Tel: 746-2798.
Prompt service and delicious cuisine.

Restoran 123, 159 Jalan Ampang. Tel: 261-4746.
Serves Chinese-style seafood under a thatched roof. Recommended especially for its Sri Lankan crabs.

Bangsar Seafood Restaurant, Lot 43873, Jalan Telawi 4, Bangsar Baru. Tel: 255-7252.
Good variety and reasonable prices.

Hai Peng Restaurant, Lot KS-5, Taman Evergreen, 4-1/2 mile, Jalan Klang. Tel: 782-5072.
This place is best known for prawns and crabs.

Continental

Le Coq D'Or, 121 Jalan Ampang. Tel: 242-9732.
One of the oldest establishments in the city, located in Bok House built in 1930. The colonial architecture has been preserved, along with the old lamps and ceiling fans, and some interesting figurines and busts. Even the waiters are a throwback of the old attentive men garbed in white. A nice quiet place for a fairly good meal.

Bistro Tabasat, Mi Casa Hotel Apartments, 368-B, Jalan Tun Razak. Tel: 261-8833.
Good barbecue buffet dinners.

Castell Grill, 81 Jalan Bukit Bintang. Tel: 242-8328.
Reputed as an up-market steak joint with a limited menu. The ribeye is especially good here.

The Ship, Jalan Sultan Ismail. Tel: 241-8805.
The thematic decor of this place lives up to its name, and wooden fittings, fishing nets and other memorabilia are attractively used to resemble a ship. A good range of food offered.

New Copper Grill, Menara Promet, Jalan Sultan Ismail. Tel: 248-5912.
A cosy little steak and fish restaurant.

Coliseum Cafe, 98 Jalan Tuanku Abdul Rahman. Tel: 292-6270.
Another old restaurant where the tablecloths are starched stiff and match the waiters' white outfits. A pervasive musty smell greets you as you enter and the place looks run-down for want of maintenance. The food, however, is tasty and cheap. The steaks and pork chops are especially recommended.

Jake's Charbroil Steaks, 21 Jalan Setiapuspa. Tel: 254-5677.

La Terrasse, 388 Jalan Tun Razak. Tel: 248-4243.
A tastefully decorated restaurant within a colonial-type house. Has a good salad and pasta bar and delicious desserts.

Troika Restaurant, Kompleks Kewangan, Jalan Raja Chulan. Tel: 261-6734.
An upmarket place where the specialities include sizzling shaslik of beef or lamb.

Caleo's Restorante Italiano, 1 Jalan Pinang. Tel: 241-0080. Has a wine bar on the first floor where pizza is served.

Memory Lane, 1st floor, Annexe Block, Menara Apera ULG, Jalan Raja Chulan. Tel: 261-5448.
Good steaks.

Hawker Food

This is something no visitor should miss while in Kuala Lumpur. Not only do hawkers dish up a good variety of authentic local dishes, the prices are also cheaper and hawker-stall dining is an experience on its own.

Although roadside stalls are a common sight, the modernisation of K.L. has also swept many of these hawkers into the concrete, air-conditioned ambience of shopping malls in which food arcades offer both local hawker fare and Western fast food. These include:

Medan Hang Tuah, 4th floor of The Mall.
A wide variety of local food sold in surroundings recreated to resemble K.L. in the 1930s, including a mock fishing village.

Hawker's Centre, Sungai Wang Plaza.
Mainly Malay and Chinese food.

Food Court, Top Floor, Kota Raya Shopping Complex.
A good mix of local fare.

Central Market. All types of local and fast food here.

Semua House, Basement, Jalan Masjid India.
All types of local food sold here.

Imbi Plaza, Basement, Jalan Imbi.
Food from all the Malaysian states can be found here.

Open-air hawker centres are sprinkled all over the city and some of the larger ones are in Bangsar, Petaling Street, Jalan Alor, Brickfields, Chow Kit, Jalan Kampung Attap (near the Badminton Hall), along Jalan Imbi and Jalan SS2 in Petaling Jaya. Food vendors also group together in shop lots on every other street.

Most hawkers keep going till 2 or 3 a.m. and some even keep their stalls open till dawn.

Guaranteed to quench your thirst

Shopping

Kuala Lumpur is fast catching up with Singapore, Hong Kong and Bangkok as a shopper's paradise. It also offers some marvellous opportunities to collectors and bargain hunters. Worthwhile finds range from antiques and rare imported spices to religious icons and metalware. Remember that bargaining is an integral part of most purchases so prepare to haggle.

Handicraft

One would have thought that gold fabric was a creation of Grecian fables. Well in Malaysia, it is grounded in reality, and it is called *songket*. Handed down from the courts of Kelantan and Pattani, this cloth is a display of dramatic handwoven tradition featuring intricate tapestry inlaid with gold and metallic thread. Women on the East Coast of Malaysia still use the traditional two-paddle floor looms to painstakingly interlace threads, with the choicest, handsomest pieces coming from Kelantan. It comes in primary colours that offset the rich tapestries. Its richness makes it more suitable for formal and ceremonial attire. It also makes stunning jackets and can be found on handbags and shoes.

Batik, the less glamourous cousin of *songket*, has more appeal

Browse around for an antique

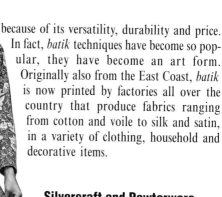

because of its versatility, durability and price. In fact, *batik* techniques have become so popular, they have become an art form. Originally also from the East Coast, *batik* is now printed by factories all over the country that produce fabrics ranging from cotton and voile to silk and satin, in a variety of clothing, household and decorative items.

Silvercraft and Pewterware

Kelantan silvercraft is one of the most successful cottage industries in Malaysia. It is a craft of fine workmanship, whether in filigree, where ornamental wire is shaped into delicate tracery, or repousses, where sheet silver is hammered into relief. All sorts of items are produced, from brooches and other jewellery to serving dishes and tableware.

Kuala Lumpur's own home-grown handicraft, **pewterware**, enjoys a worldwide reputation for its stylish and attractive handmade designs. Pewter is an alloy of tin mixed with a little copper and antimony. Produced with traditional methods of casting and soldering used by the founder 100 years ago, but in modern designs, pewterware has an elegance all its own. The hardness of the metal gives it durability, and its silvery finish makes caring for it so much easier. There are hundreds of items ranging from tableware, candelabra and ornamental pieces to lapel pins, figurines and Garfield pendants.

Kites and Tops

The traditional *wau* and *gasing* (kites and tops) for which the East Coast is best known enjoy international popularity. Both are traditional sports, and kite flying especially dates back to the 1500s.

The *wau* comes in all shapes and sizes. The most popular and the largest is the *wau bulan* or moon kite, which measures 3½ metres (11½ ft) from head to tail and is capable of soaring to great heights. Its wooden frame is covered with stiff parchment and adorned with gay coloured streamers. Smaller versions are made as decorative items.

Top spinning is no child's play either, not when the traditional Malay top is about the size of a dinner plate and weighs as much as 5½ kilogrammes (12 pounds). The tops are usually disc shaped, and are carefully balanced for spinning power. A good top can spin for two hours at a stretch.

Cane, Bamboo and Woven Straw Products, and Beadwork

These are bountiful in Malaysia, though the more traditional form of bamboo-weaving belongs to the East Coast. Cane and wicker are turned into furniture and household items. *Mengkuang* (pandanas) leaves are woven into mats, baskets, hats and decorative items, and split bamboo strips are shaped into trays, baskets and food covers.

In Sarawak, nipah palm reeds are woven into decorative mats,  and rattan skins are used to make mats and baskets of exceptional durability. A good mat is said to last up to 30 years. Beadwork, traditional to the Dayaks, an indigenous people in Sarawak, is extremely attractive when done on headbands, necklaces, belts, food covers and baskets.

Clothing

Good quality cottons, either locally made or imported, are popular and fashioned into all forms of clothing. Other materials are also available and tailoring is reasonably priced.

Miscellaneous

Cameras, pens, watches and mini-compos are cheap since they are exempted from import duty, but leather and imported electronic goods are expensive.

Where to buy it

The best of Malaysian handicraft items, unfortunately, are found not in K.L., but in their homestates. **Handicraft Centre**, in the city,

A CLASS OF ITS OWN

Along Bukit Bintang

however, markets almost all traditional handicraft. A good variety can be found at **Infokraf** along Jalan Raja and **Karyaneka**, along Jalan Raja Chulan.

Pewterware can be purchased almost anywhere but **Selangor Pewter's** showroom along Jalan Tuanku Abdul Rahman displays the entire range and also takes special orders.

There are many shops that sell *batik* and *songket* besides **Batik Malaysia** in Jalan Tun Perak, and it is a good idea to look around those in the **Jalan Tuanku Abdul Rahman** and **Masjid India** areas, as well as the bazaars in **Kampung Baru** and **Jalan Raja Laut**. Shops in Masjid India, Jalan Melayu and Lorong Bugus also sell textiles, clothes, religious paraphernalia, metalware and handicraft from other countries as well, including India, Pakistan, Afghanistan, Middle East and Indonesia. One can find value-for-money items with some browsing in these specialty shops.

Chinatown naturally, is the place for China-imported goods such as herbs, spices and Taoist prayer items. Equally ubiquitous are the shops and sidewalk vendors that stock cheap clothing, shoes, toys, crockery and other household items. Cottons especially are worth buying here, albeit their fake brand names.

For better quality and designer labels, the best bet would be the large shopping complexes. Those in the Bukit Bintang area, such as **Sungai Wang, Jalan Bukit Bintang** and **K.L. Plaza, Ampang Park** along Ampang Road, **The Oval** along Jalan Raja Chulan and **The Mall** on Jalan Putra, house department stores and boutiques with a range of clothes and other goods. **Yow Chuan Plaza** on Jalan Ampang is the upmarket joint, and **Imbi Plaza** in Bukit Bintang, the centre for computer and electronic buffs.

Snacks galore

Calendar of Special Events

The ethnic mix in Malaysia – a mash of Malays, Chinese, Indians, Eurasians and 30 other races – weaves a cultural fabric embroidered with tradition, variety and colour. Auspicious occasions and festivals of religious and cultural significance of each race are spread out through the year. In consonance with different calendar systems, there are three "new year" celebrations in addition to January 1, social festivities like harvest festivals and a plethora of Muslim, Christian, Hindu, Buddhist, Taoist religious occasions.

Malaysians, holding dear to tradition, observe these auspicious festivities with "open house", which means that they invite all their friends who are not celebrating that particular festivity to their homes to indulge in that great Malaysian pastime: eating. Open house is probably the most egalitarian tradition in Malaysia in that everyone practises it – from the humblest man on the street to the highest echelons of power. Malaysians whom you befriend during your visit would invite you to their homes on these occasions.

Here is the schedule of major festivals in 1991.

January 30 1991: *Thaipusam* commemorates the birth of the Hindu deity, Lord Subramaniam, and is celebrated by Hindus all over the country with the fervour of the Mardi Gras. Thousands converge at the holiest Hindu shrine at Batu Caves to offer thanksgiving and penance, many of them bearing the *kavadi*, a wooden-frame structure designed to carry containers of milk and rose water, to be propitiated as offerings. Sometimes the *kavadi* takes on a somewhat macabre dimension, with spears and skewers pierced into the body of the bearer.

Deities adorn the walls of Sri Mahamariaman Hindu Temple

The crowds start gathering the evening before when the statue of Subramaniam is drawn by chariot from the Sri Mahamariaman Temple on Jalan Bandar to the temple cave. *Kavadi*-bearers generally begin their 272-step climb at dawn, so get there early, though the festivities go on throughout the day. Taxis and buses ply the route from the city centre, and there is also a train service specially for the day departing from the K.L. Railway Station. A field day for shutterbugs.

February 1: City Day. Kuala Lumpur brings out the fireworks, streamers and balloons to celebrate its birthday, and special events, from open-air cultural and musical performances to sea sports, take place throughout the day.

February 15-16: Chinese New Year heralds the first moon of the lunar new year, and is marked by prayers, reunion dinners, lion dances, to the accompaniment of huge drums, gongs and fire crackers. Both days are public holidays but some shops close for as many as five to seven days. Chinatown is at its best in the run-up to the celebration. Join the crowds in their last-minute shopping on Chinese New Year's Eve at Jalan Petaling and sample some of the exquisite sweetmeats imported from China for the occasion.

April 16-17: *Hari Raya Puasa*, the occasion of the first day of the Muslim month of Shawal, follows a month of fasting called Ramadan. Muslims usher in the day by attending prayers with open house.

May 28: *Vesak Day*, the most significant festival for Buddhists, commemorates the birth, enlightenment and death of the Buddha. Temples are packed with devotees offering prayers, giving alms to the monks and releasing pigeons. Visit the International Buddhist Pagoda on Jalan Berhala, Brickfields, or the temple along Jalan Gasing in Petaling Jaya. Buy incense from a vendor and follow the procession through the motions of lighting and placing joss sticks in the large sand-filled urns, then clasping hands together and bowing to the statue of Buddha. If you wish, you could receive a yellow string from a monk or nun to be worn around the wrist for luck.

August 31: Malaysia's National Day, the highlight of Independence day or Hari Merdeka, is a mammoth parade at Merdeka Square at Jalan Raja. The parade starts in the morning, at 7 or 8 a.m. It is normally difficult to find a good spot to view it unless you go to the Merdeka

1990 National Day parade

Square grounds very early. Be warned though, that roads in the immediate vicinity are closed to traffic. You can, however, watch the live telecast from your hotel room.

November 5: *Deepavali*, the festival of lights, falls in the Tamil month of Aipassi. Indians observe the triumph of good over evil with prayers, and line their gardens with oil lamps. Another open house affair.

December 25: Christmas is celebrated as it is the world over, with Santa, decorated trees, carolling and midnight mass. Shopping complexes and hotels take the lead with their decorations, complete with sleighs and canned snow. The Malaysian spirit prevails so open house is the order of the day.

Right, National Day light-up

What to Know?
Practical Information

TRAVEL ESSENTIALS

When To Visit

Kuala Lumpur is sunny, steamy and sometimes salubrious. Daytime temperatures can reach 33°C (92°F); the nights can be balmy, with the temperature dropping by as much as 10°C (14°F), although most times, the difference is slight. Humidity hovers above 80 percent and remians high throughout the year.

As the city has no defined seasonal weather pattern, a visit can be planned for any time of the year. The central mountain range keeps out the worst of the north-east monsoon (November to February), and the city's inland location protects it from the south-west monsoon (July to September). Kuala Lumpur gets its share of heavy rain though, with downpours likely in the afternoon.

Visas

Tourist visas can be extended by applying at the **Immigration Department** at Block 1, Pusat Bandar Damansara, Damansara Heights (8 a.m. to 4.15 p.m., Monday to Friday; 8 a.m. to 12.45 p.m., Saturday). Fee: M$5.

Except for Indian nationals, Commonwealth citizens and those of British protectorates: the Republic of Ireland, Switzerland, the Netherlands, San Marino and Lichtenstein, do not need visas.

Visitors from Australia, Belgium, Denmark, Finland, Iceland, Italy, Korea, Japan, Norway, Sweden, the United States and West Germany are allowed to stay three months without a visa.

Citizens of ASEAN nations can stay for one month without a visa.

All tourists, in transit or otherwise, are allowed a 14-day visa-free visit, except those from Albania, Cambodia, China, India, Israel, Laos, Mongolia, Republic of Transkei, South Africa, Taiwan, Vietnam and Zimbabwe.

Citizens of Bulgaria, Czechoslovakia, East Germany, Hungary, Poland, Rumania, the Soviet Union and Yugoslavia are allowed a seven-day visa-free social visit.

Vaccinations

A yellow fever vaccination is required if arriving from an infected country.

Money Matters

Malaysian currency comprises the *Ringgit* (dollar), which is worth 100 *sen* (cents). Banknotes come in eight denominations: M$1 (blue), M$5 (green), M$10 (red), M$20 (brownish-orange), M$50 (bluish-green), M$100 (purple), M$500 (orange) and M$1,000 (dark green).

There are also one-dollar coins. Coins are needed for public phones at 10 *sen* per local call, driver-operated ticket dispensers in mini-buses and vending machines. However, one-dollar notes are accepted by most mini-buses as well.

Card-operated public phones are common in most places around Kuala Lumpur. These phones make use of pre-paid phone cards which can be purchased at selected stores such as the 7-Eleven convenience chain. If you intend to make out-of-town calls, these cards are particularly useful since they obviate the necessity of digging into your wallet each time the "your three minutes are up" beep starts intruding upon your telephone conversation.

The *ringgit* was rated at M$2.70 to US$1 in early 1990. For daily rates, check the business sections of almost all local newspapers.

Money changers can be found all over the city; their rates vary quite a bit, though they offer better exchange rates than the banks. Hotels give rates slightly lower than those at banks.

Traveller's cheques are accepted at major hotels, restaurants and department stores, although banks will give you the best rates. American Express, Diner's Club, Mastercard and Visa credit cards are widely accepted throughout Kuala Lumpur.

Clothing

Clothes should be light and loose. Pack mostly cottons and other natural fibres, rather than synthetics.

Sunglasses are essential, and suntan lotion and sun block are advisable for bare skin. Shoes should be removed when entering a place of worship or a home, so slip-ons or sandals are handy.

Electricity

Power supply is 220 or 240 volts at 50 Hz, and most outlets use three-pin, flat-pronged plugs. Equipment using 110 volts will require a transformer.

Airport Tax

A tax of M$15 is levied at the airport at departure. Malaysian Airlines adds the tax to the price of tickets bought in Malaysia; other airlines do not.

GETTING ACQUAINTED

Geography

Malaysia's landmass of 330,434 sq km (127,000 sq miles) covers the peninsula and a third of Borneo Island. It is one of the world's largest producers of tin, rubber and palm oil, in addition to producing substantial amounts of petroleum, pepper and tropical hardwoods. On the manufacturing side, the country is also the world's largest exporter of semi-conductors, examination gloves and condoms and the second largest exporter of air-conditioners.

Its 15.6 million population comprises mostly Malays, Dayaks, Muruts, Bidayuhs, Kadazans and about 30 other races of Melano-Polynesian stock, followed by substantial numbers of immigrant races such as the Chinese, Indians, Portuguese, Eurasians and others. The Chinese are largely Cantonese and Hokkiens, with a liberal sprinkling of Hakkas; the Indians consist mainly of Tamils, followed by prominent communities of Malayali, Punjabi and Sindhi descent.

Kuala Lumpur, the nation's capital, is situated about halfway down the west coast of the peninsula and 35 km (21.7 miles) inland. Dubbed Malaysia's Garden City of Lights, it started as a riverine trading post at the confluence of the Klang and Gombak rivers some 130 years ago. It has since grown to a metropolis with an area of about 234 sq km (89 sq miles) and some two million inhabitants.

Passport photos

Climate

Kuala Lumpur's climate is quite constant all year round despite the monsoon seasons – November to February (east coast) and July to September (west coast). Temperatures range from 21 - 33°C (73 - 92°F), and humidity is on the high side of 80 percent. Mean annual rainfall is 220 cm (90 inches).

Time

Kuala Lumpur is +8 hours GMT and +16 US Pacific Standard Time.

How Not To Offend

Shoes should be removed before entering a Malaysian home or place of worship. When in a mosque, visitors should put on a robe, which will be provided, and ensure their limbs are covered. Women should also cover their heads, therefore a scarf is always handy. Pointing with the forefinger, pointing you feet a t

a person or touching his head are considered rude in almost all of multi-racial Malaysia's cultures.

Whom Do You Trust?

For the foreigner, Kuala Lumpur is generally free of crime. However, as in most countries, it is sensible to take reasonable precautions against pickpockets.

Tipping

All service establishments such as hotels, restaurants, bars and clubs add a service charge to bills, so tipping is not necessary. Taxis expect the exact meter fare and nothing more.

Tourist Information

The **Malaysian Tourist Development Corporation** headquarters is on the 26th floor, Menara Dato Onn, Putra World Trade Centre, Jalan Tun Ismail, Tel: 293-5188.

Tourist information centres at:

Putra World Trade Centre
Level 2
Jalan Tun Ismail
Tel: 441-1295

Information counter
Kuala Lumpur Railway Station
Tel: 274-6063

Kuala Lumpur Tourist Information Centre
Jalan Parlimen
Tel: 293-6664

Arrival Hall
Terminal 1
Subang International Airport
Tel: 746-5707

Malaysia Tourist Information Complex
109 Jalan Ampang
Tel: 243-4929

Kuala Lumpur Visitors Centre
Jalan Sultan Hishamuddin
Tel: 238-1832

There is also a **24-hour tourist hotline** to help tourists and answer queries. Tel: 291-9191.

For details of **current and special events** in the city, call City Hall's information service at 292-2722. And for the daily weather forecast, telephone 1052.

GETTING AROUND

Taxis

Kuala Lumpur's taxis are conspicuously painted yellow and black or red and white. They offer a convenient and quite economical means of moving around the

course and are necessary in order to take a taxi to any part of the city or the suburbs, and should be handed to the driver at the end of the journey. The same applies at the railway station. Coupons to various destinations in the city and its vicinity are available on Platform 4.

city, and drivers usually speak at least a smattering of English. Malaysian cabbies are proud of their credibility and occasionally make news headlines with acts of honesty. Once befriended, they can make charming conversationalists.

Air-conditioning and fare meters are compulsory in all taxis. Make sure the meter is activated when boarding. Rates are M$1 for the first 2 km (1.2 miles) and 10 cents for each additional 200 metres (660 ft) or per six seconds.

It is fairly easy to get a taxi either by queueing at taxi stands, flagging one down by the roadside or ordering by phone. Try to avoid hailing one between 3 and 3.30 p.m., as cabbies change shifts around this time and usually do not pick up passengers unless you happen to be going their way. There is a surcharge of M$1 for ordering a cab by phone. There is also a 50 percent surcharge on the meter fare between midnight and 6 a.m. And if there are more than two passengers per taxi, an additional 10 cents per additional passenger is levied. No tipping is required.

It is also possible to hire a taxi by the hour. Rates vary. Some taxi companies charge a flat rate of M$15 per hour, others add on M$9 to the meter fare.

Taxi coupons at fixed rates are available to travellers on arrival at Kuala Lumpur International Airport. These coupons can be purchased at a booth at the airport con-

Buses

The city's bus service comes in the form of stage buses and mini buses. Fares on the big buses are calculated at the rate of 20 cents for the first kilometre (0.62 miles) and 5 cents for each additional kilometre. Check with the conductor about fares for your destination and have loose change ready. There is a standard fare of 50 cents on all mini buses plying the routes in and around Kuala Lumpur. Routes are zonal and bus stops indicate the zones and areas. Many of these buses have driver-operated ticket machines, so have coins on hand as no change is dispensed. Both bus services end at midnight. Booklets on bus routes are sold at most bookshops for about M$3.

Limousines

Most hotels have air-conditioned limousine services, and prices vary, but some are comparable with taxi rates, especially to the airport and suburbs.

Rental cars

For between M$25 and M$45 per hour, one can see the city in style in a chauffeured Mercedes offered by Avis, Hertz and a number of local car rental agencies. For self-drive cars, rentals range from M$108 to M$165 per day, with an additional M$12 for car insurance and M$5 for personal insurance (optional), plus petrol costs (M$1.05 per litre for premium at the time of publication).

Maps

The Tourist Development Corporation's map and guide of Kuala Lumpur is available at any TDC information counter and in most hotels. The map shows all routes, landmarks and bus stops within the city centre. Petrol stations sell detailed road maps for the entire country but these would be useful only to motorists.

WHERE TO STAY

Hotels

The list below is by no means exhaustive. Hotels listed here are grouped according to their lowest priced rooms, rather than the standard of facilities and service provided. The prices noted are for the least-

expensive single room and the most expensive suite for each hotel. All hotels are fully air-conditioned and have restaurants. The more expensive ones have pools, health clubs, sports facilities and shopping arcades. Asterisks (*) denote hotels whose room price includes tax and service charge. For all others, add 10 percent service charge and 5 percent government tax.

MS$200 and up

Kuala Lumpur Hilton
Jalan Sultan Ismail
Tel: 242-2222
M$260-$2,750/night
Five-star property, recently refurbished, and most well-known for its discotheque, the Tin Mine.

Ming Court
Lot 2, Section 43,
Jalan Ampang
Tel: 261-8888
M$220-M$2,500/night
Caters largely to business travellers and is located within an office neighbourhood.

Pan Pacific
Jalan Putra
Tel: 442-5555
* M$299-$2,000/night
Although a bit out of the general town area, this hotel is close to the convention complex, Putra World Trade Centre and the shopping area of Chow Kit bazaar.

Parkroyal Kuala Lumpur
54, Jalan Sultan Ismail
Tel: 242-5588
M$225-$2,200/night
An old property recently given a facelift. In the heart of the city.

Park Avenue
16 Jalan Imbi
Tel: 242-8333
M$225-M$1,380/night (nett)
Just a short while away from the main entertainment hubs of Bukit Bintang, this hotel is famous for its bubble lift which offers a panoramic view of Kuala Lumpur.

Regent of Kuala Lumpur
160 Jalan Bukit Bintang
Tel: 241-8000
M$265-$6,000/night
K.L.'s newest hotel, a polished monument with fine service; at the head of Jalan Bukit Bintang.

Shangri-La
11 Jalan Sultan Ismail
Tel: 232-2388
M$300-$3,000/night
Centrally located in the business district and famed for its cuisine.

M$100-$199

Equatorial
Jalan Sultan Ismail
Tel: 261-2022
* M$168-$1,200/night
Its coffee lounge, the Blue Moon, pipes through nostalgic music from 1930s and 1940s.

Federal Hotel
35 Jalan Bukit Bintang
Tel: 248-9166
M$140-$800/night

The oldest five-star property in Malaysia, strategically located in the heart of Bukit Bintang.

Fortuna
87 Jalan Berangan
Tel: 241-9111
* M$110-$185/night
Small but central; within a quiet neighbourhood just behind the main Bukit Bintang area.

Holiday Inn on the Park
Jalan Pinang
Tel: 248-1066
* M$173-$1,500/night
Malaysia's first Holiday Inn, this is close to a lot of upmarket entertainment establishments.

Merlin Kuala Lumpur
2 Jalan Sultan Ismail
Tel: 248-0033
* M$120-$340/night
One of K.L.'s largest and oldest hotels; a 10-minute taxi ride to most shopping and entertainment places.

M$50-$99

Apollo
106 Jalan Bukit Bintang
Tel: 242-8133
* M$55.20-$100/night
Medium-class hotel close to shopping malls.

Hotel Malaya
Jalan Hang Lekir
Tel: 232-7722
* M$90.85-$253/night
In central Chinatown, surrounded by lots of shopping areas.

Kuala Lumpur Mandarin
2 Jalan Sultan
Tel: 230-3000

* M$69-$241/night
Also in the heart of Chinatown, close
to major bus and taxi terminals and
the Central Market cultural centre.
Its health centre is reputed to be
among the best in K.L.

The Lodge
2 Jalan Tengah
Off Jalan Sultan Ismail
Tel: 242-0122
* M$86.25 - M$97.75/night
Right opposite the K.L. Hilton and
close to shopping areas; an excellent
choice for the budget traveller.

Malaysia Hotel
67 - 69, Jalan Bukit Bintang
Tel: 242-8033
* M$69/night
A medium-class hotel right along
Jalan Bukit Bintang.

Plaza Hotel
Jalan Raja Laut
Tel: 298-2255
* M$90-M$350/night
Close to the Chow Kit shopping
bazaar and the Pan Pacific Hotel.

Kuala Lumpur Station Hotel
Jalan Sultan Hishamuddin
Tel: 274-7433
* M$43.70-$55.20/night
This is for those who like a colonial
atmosphere of high ceilings, languid
fans, spacious rooms with wicker
furniture.

Under M$50

Chamtan Hotel
62 Jalan Masjid India
Tel: 293-0144
* M$48.30-$69.30/night
Surrounded by excellent shopping
places in the Jalan Tuanku Abdul
Rahman district, though entertain-
ment is limited.

City Hotel
366 Jalan Raja Laut
Tel: 441-4466
* M$43-$66.50/night
A reasonably-prized establishment
near the Chow Kit area.

Youth Hostels

KL International Youth Hostel
Jalan Kampung Atap
Tel: 230-6780
* M$12/night

MAYC Complex
40 Jalan Syed Putra
Tel: 274-6262
* M$50-$75/night

Wisma Belia
Jalan Syed Putra
Tel: 274-4833
* M$50-$90/night

Guest Houses

Many small hotels housed in shop units, can be found in parts of the city especially along Jalan Tuanku Abdul Rahman and in the Chow Kit and Bukit Bintang areas. Better known by their old Malay name, *rumah tumpangan* (which means lodging houses), some of them are quite reputable. For example, the Merdeka Hotel, in Jalan Raja Muda, offers decent and clean rooms at prices lower than those of budget hotels. Room rates range from M$15 to M$30.

HOURS OF BUSINESS AND PUBLIC HOLIDAYS

Business hours

Business hours are from 8.30 a.m. or 9 a.m., Monday to Friday. Many businesses are open on Saturdays from 8.30 a.m. or 9 a.m. to 12.30 p.m. or 1 p.m. Government offices are open from 8 a.m. to 4.15 p.m Monday through Friday, and from 8 a.m. to 12.45 p.m. on Saturday.

Banks open six days a week: 10 a.m. to 3 p.m. on weekdays, and 9.30 a.m. to 11.30 p.m. on Saturday.

Post offices open from 8 a.m. to 4.30 p.m., six days a week. The General Post Office is at Menara Dayabumi, Jalan Sultan Hishamuddin. Most hotels will mail letters for you and sell stamps at the reception desk. Some of the smaller bookstores in the city also sell stamps.

Almost all department stores, supermarkets and shopping complexes are open from 10 a.m. to 10 p.m., seven days a week. Many of the shops along Jalan Tuanku Abdul Rahman and Jalan Masjid India, close at 6.30 p.m. or 7.30 p.m.

Public Holidays

The following are official public holidays in Kuala Lumpur in 1991:

New Year's Day: January 1

City Day: February 1

Chinese New Year: February 15-16

Hari Raya Puasa: April 16-17

Labour Day: May 1

Vesak Day: May 28

H.M. the King's Birthday: June 5

Hari Raya Haji: June 13

National Day: August 31

Prophet Muhammad's Birthday: October 1

Deepavali: November 5

Christmas Day: December 25

HEALTH AND EMERGENCIES

Hygiene

Tap water is perfectly safe for drinking. Those unfortunate enough to have experienced that scourge of travellers – Delhi belly, Cairo curd

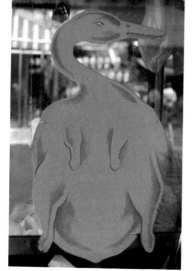

or Montezuma's revenge – will be relieved to know Malaysian piped water is treated and unlikely to cause stomach upsets. Restaurants and other eating establishments offer boiled water.

Food served in licensed restaurants and at hawker stalls is clean and hygienically prepared. Avoid unlicensed hawker areas, since hygienic standards in these areas are bound to be somewhat slack and could cause stomach upsets and intestinal disorders.

Pharmacies are found in shopping complexes and the city's business areas. They are well-stocked and have registered pharmacists to attend to customers' needs. Controlled drugs are sold only on prescription.

Health Emergencies

Many hotels have doctors on call to treat emergencies. Kuala Lumpur has a good number of hospitals offering excellent medical care. Both government and private hospitals have fully-equipped emergency and intensive care units to cope with any medical crisis.

Hospitals

The **General Hospital** at Jalan Pahang, tel: 292-1044, and the **Universiti Hospital** at Jalan Universiti in suburban Petaling Jaya, emergency tel: 756-4422 ext 2500, are government owned. **Private hospitals** include:
Tawakal Specialist Centre at 192-A, Jalan Pahang, tel: 423-3599;
Tung Shin Hospital at 102, Jalan Pudu, tel: 238-8900;
CHM Medical Centre at 106, Jalan Pudu, tel: 238-2055;
Pantai Medical Centre at 8, Jalan Bukit Pantai, tel: 757-5077;
Subang Medical Centre at 1, Jalan SS12/1A Subang Jaya, tel: 734-1212;
Assunta Hospital at Jalan Templer in Petaling Jaya, tel: 792-3433.

Medical and Dental Clinics

There are many 24-hour polyclinics, or the privately-owned specialist clinics, which offer specialist treatment in the city. Registered medical practitioners are listed in the Yellow Pages of the telephone directory. So are qualified dental surgeons.

Police Emergencies

The emergency number for police, ambulance and fire in Kuala Lumpur is 999.

There is also a **tourist police unit** specially set up to assist travellers. They can be reached at the city's police headquarters in Jalan Hang Tuah or on their 24-hour phone line: 243-5522.

Emergency Repairs

Sidewalk cobblers and key grinders are standard features on almost every other street downtown and in shopping complexes. These tradesmen do a pretty good job of mending shoes and bags at fairly low prices. Some of them are jacks-of-all-trades: rubber stamps, signs, engraving and so forth.

COMMUNICATIONS AND NEWS

Telecommunications and Postal Services

Telephone, telegram, mail, telex and FAX facilities are offered by most hotels, and in the case of luxury hotels, IDD (international direct dial) phones are available in guest rooms.

International calls can also be made at any Kedai Telekom (Telecoms shops) in the city during office hours. A 24-hour service is available at the Central Telecoms Building in Jalan Raja Chulan.

Shipping

Larger shops will handle documentation and shipping for purchases, or will recommend handling agents to do the job.

Post offices sell boxes for goods being sent by mail.

News Media

The two largest selling English dailies in Malaysia are *The Star* (morning tabloid) and *The New Straits Times* (morning broadsheet). Both offer fairly comprehensive coverage of local and foreign news. The *Asian Wall Street Journal*, *International Herald Tribune* and *USA Today* can be obtained at most newsstands and bookshops, which also stock an extensive range of local and international magazines and periodicals. Some shops also offer newspapers such as the *Daily Mirror* and *The Times* from England, and dailies from the United States, Australia, Bangkok, Tokyo and other parts of the world.

Radio Ibu Kota (Voice of the Capital City) is a special service for Kuala Lumpur and has programmes for visitors and travellers. It is broadcast by the government-owned Radio Television Malaysia on 97.2 MHz. FM radio includes varied English-language musical programmes from classical to jazz and pop. RTM also broadcasts an English service called Radio Four Network that begins at 6 a.m. daily and ends at midnight, with English-language news bulletins in the mornings at 6.30 a.m., 7 a.m. and 8 a.m.; in the afternoons at 1.30 p.m.; and in the evenings at 6.30 p.m., 8 p.m., 9:30 p.m. and 11 p.m.

News Round-Up

Here is a summary of happenings in Malaysia in recent months: Datuk Seri Dr Mahathir Mohammed is the country's fourth Prime Minister since Independence, and of late, has been seriously challenged by an opposition group led by the Spirit of '46 movement together with the Democratic Action Party. Dr Mahathir, who came to power in 1981, heads a coalition government made up of over 10 component parties.

Malaysia spearheads an environmental consciousness movement among Third World countries, especially those in the Commonwealth. This was a direct result of the Commonwealth Heads of States meeting held in Kuala Lumpur in October 1989.

The nation also plays an major role in the world anti-narcotics movement. The Prime Minister is the head of the UN Commission of Drug Abuse. In addition, Malaysia has instituted what amounts to the most draconian anti-drug legislation in

the world: mandatory death sentence for the possession of 15 grammes and above, of heroin.

1990 was **Visit Malaysia Year**, designed to make tourism an even bigger contributor to the national coffers. The government expected 4.3 million tourists by the end of the year, with projected earnings of M$2.5 billion.

SPORTS

Almost all hotels that charge M$100 and above per night, have swimming pools; those above M$200 also have health clubs, tennis and squash courts.

Swimming

Public pools at **Jalan Raja Chulan**, tel: 248-3110; **Bangsar Sports Complex** (tel: 254-6065); and **Chin Woo Stadium** (tel: 232-4602); are open from 9.30 a.m. or 10 a.m. to midnight. Charges are nominal.

Jogging

Taman Tasik Perdana (Lake Gardens), **Taman Tasik Titiwangsa** in Ampang, **Taman Tasik Permaisuri** in Ceras, **Taman Tunku Abdul Rahman** and **Tugu Negara** have jogging paths.

Court and Raquet Games

Sports complexes in and around the city offer facilities for badminton, tennis, squash, volleyball, table tennis and *sepak takraw*. These courts are open from 7 or 8 a.m. till 11 p.m. or midnight. **Bangsar Sports Complex** (tel: 254-6065); **Kampung Datuk Keramat** (tel: 456-4853); **Taman Tasik Titiwangsa** (tel: 423-9558); **Bandar Tun Razak Sports Complex** (tel: 930-8935); **Jalan Tun Razak Multi-purpose Hall** (tel: 242-6467); and **National Sports Council Complex** (tel: 254-8211).

Bowling

Bowling alleys at **Federal Hotel**, Jalan Bukit Bintang, **Wisma Mirama** on the 5th Floor, and **Yow Chuan Plaza**.

Golf

Awana, 45 minutes from K.L. and on the way to Genting Highlands, is a 21-hole golf-course. **Morib**, an hour's drive south-west of K.L. has a nine-hole course. Nearer the city is the **Saujana Golf and Country Club**, located near the airport, with a 36-hole golf course. At Sungai Buloh is the **Rahman Putra Golf and Country Club**. Many of the clubs within the city charge green fees for non-members.

SPECIAL INFORMATION

The Malay language

The Malay language, or *Bahasa Malaysia*, is polysyllabic, with variations in syllables conveying changes in meaning, unlike tonal languages such as Mandarin and Thai. For example, *duduk* (sit) is a verb. By adding the prefix *ke* and suffix *an,* we get the noun *kedudukan*, which means position. By adding a different prefix, *pen*, we get another noun, *penduduk*, which means inhabitant. Adding an *i* after *duduk* turns it into an active verb (to sit), while *menduduk* is a present continuous verb.

Tones do not vary to give different meanings and, for the most part, words are pronounced as they are spelt. In general, the pronunciation is the same as in English, with a few exceptions.

In *Bahasa Malaysia*, "a" is pronounced "ar" as in Arlington or tar. The letter "e" has an "er" sound, as in reserve. You will also find that "c" is pronounced "ch" as in chair; the letter "g" is always hard, as in gun and garden, not as in ginger; and "sy" is pronounced "sh".

The language uses two distinct scripts: *Jawi* and *Rumi*. *Jawi* is the Arabic form of writing; *Rumi* the Roman alphabet, considered the easier of the two and also the official script of the country.

Here is a small vocabulary to get you on your way.

Numbers

One
Satu

Two
Dua

98

Three
Tiga

Four
Empat

Five
Lima

Six
Enam

Seven
Tujuh

Eight
Lapan

Nine
Sembilan

Ten
Sepuluh

Eleven
Sebelas

Twelve
Dua belas

Thirteen
Tiga belas

Twenty
Dua puluh

Twenty-one
Dua puluh satu

One hundred
Seratus

Two hundred
Dua ratus

One thousand
Seribu

Days of the week

Monday
Isnin

Tuesday
Selasa

Wednesday
Rabu

Thursday
Khamis

Friday
Jumaat

Saturday
Sabtu

Sunday
Ahad

Today
Hari ini

Yesterday
Kelmarin

Tomorrow
Esok

Greetings and others

How do you do?
Apa Khabar?

Good morning
Selamat pagi

Good afternoon
Selamat petang

Good evening
Selamat malam

Goodbye
Selamat tinggal

Bon voyage
Selamat jalan

Fine/good
Baik

Thank you
Terima kasih

Please
Tolong/sila

Excuse me
Maafkan saya

I am sorry
Saya minta maaf

Yes
Ya

No
Tidak

Pronouns

I
Saya

You
Anda/awak

He/she
Dia

We
Kami

They
Mereka

Forms of address

Mr
Encik

Mrs
Puan

Miss
Cik

Directions and Travel

Where
Di mana

Right
Kanan

Left
Kiri

Turn
Belok

Go
Pergi

Stop
Berhenti

Follow
Ikut

Near
Dekat

Far
Jauh

Inside
Dalam

Outside
Luar

Front
Hadapan

Behind
Belakang

Here
Sini

There
Sana

Road/street
Jalan

Lane
Lorong

Bridge
Jambatan

Junction
Simpang

One-way street
Jalan sehala

North
Utara

South
Selatan

East
Timur

West
Barat

Useful phrases

How much?
Berapa harganya?

Can you help me?
Bolehkah encik tolong saya?

Where is this place?
Di mana tempat ini?

How far?
Berapa jauh?

I want to go to...
Saya hendak pergi ke...

Stop here
Tolong berhenti sini

Expensive
Mahal

Lower the price
Kurang harganya

Too big
Besar sangat

Too small
Kecil sangat

Any other colour?
Ada warna lain?

Other handy words

Drink
Minum (verb), minuman (noun)

Eat
Makan (verb), makanan (noun)

Fruit
Buah-buahan

Water
Air

Have
Ada

Don't have
Tidak ada

Toilet
Tandas

Why?
Mengapa?

When?
Bila?

Hot (spicy)
Pedas

Hot (heat)
Panas

Cold
Sejuk

Sweet
Manis

Sour
Masam

Delicious
Sedap

Clean
Bersih

Dirty
Kotor

Beautiful
Cantik

Open
Buka

Close
Tutup

Never
Tidak pernah

Often
Selalu

Sometimes
Kadang-kadang

USEFUL ADDRESSES

Malaysian Banks

Bank Bumiputra Malaysia Berhad
Menara Bumiputra
Tel: 291-9199

Malayan Banking Berhad
Menara Maybank
100 Jalan Tun Perak
Tel: 230-8833

Perwira Habib Bank
Wisma SPK
Tel: 243-2000

Public Bank Berhad
Bangunan Public Bank
Tel: 274-1788

United Asian Bank Berhad
Menara UABB
Tel: 293-1722

United Malayan Banking Corporation
UMBC Building
Jalan Sultan Sulaiman
Tel: 230-9866, 230-5833

Overseas Banks

Algemene Bank Nederland N.V.
Wisma Sachdev
16-2 Jalan Raja Laut
Tel: 298-9155, 298-6093

Australia & New Zealand Banking Group
Wisma Genting
Tel: 261-6088, 261-6790

Bank of Nova Scotia
Menara Boustead
Tel: 241-0766

Bank of Tokyo
1 Lebuh Ampang
Tel: 238-9100, 238-5855

Banque Nationale de Paris
MUI Plaza, Jalan P. Ramlee
Tel: 248-4377, 248-4479

Barclays Bank PLC
Bangunan MIDF
Tel: 261-0354

Citibank N.A.
28 Medan Pasar
Tel: 232-5334, 232-3955

Deutsche Bank
15 Jalan Raja Chulan
Tel: 232-9455, 230-6811

Hongkong & Shanghai Bank
2 Lebuh Ampang
Tel: 230-0744, 230-9022

Manufacturers Hanover Trust
UBN Towers
Tel: 238-0766

Mitsui Bank
9th floor, Mui Plaza
Jalan P. Ramlee
Tel: 242-9544

Sanwa Bank
MUI Plaza
Jalan P. Ramlee
Tel: 2487722

Standard Chartered Bank
2 Jalan Ampang
Tel: 232-6555, 232-7766

Credit Card Offices

American Express (Malaysia)
5th floor, Bangunan MAS
Jalan Sultan Ismail

Tel: 261-3000, 261-4000 (24 hours)
Hours: 8:30 a.m. - 6 p.m., Monday
to Friday
8:30 a.m. - noon, Saturday

Diner's Club (Malaysia)
Wisma Selangor Dredging
142-B Jalan Ampang
Tel: 261-1322, 261-1055
Hours: 9 a.m. - 5 p.m., Monday to
Friday
9 a.m. - 1 p.m., Saturday

MBf Mastercard Services
12th floor, Wisma MCA
Jalan Ampang
Tel: 261-6355, 261-3144 (after
office hours)
Hours: 9 a.m. - 5 p.m., Monday to
Friday
9 a.m. - 1 p.m., Saturday

Visa Centre
Menara Maybank
7th floor, East Wing
100 Jalan Tun Perak
Tel: 230-8833
Hours: 9 a.m. - 5 p.m., Monday to
Friday
9 a.m. - 1 p.m., Saturday

Airline offices

Aeroflot Soviet Airlines
Wisma Tong Ah, 1 Jalan Perak.
Tel: 261-3231. Airport: 746-5378

Air Canada
79 Jalan Bukit Bintang
Tel: 242-4311

Air India
Bangunan Angkasa Raya,
123 Jalan Ampang
Tel: 242-0166.
Airport: 746-4805

Air Lanka
UG4, Bangunan Perangsang
Segemal, Jalan Kampung Attap
Tel: 274-0211

Alitalia
Plaza See Hoy Chan
Tel: 238-0366

America West Airlines
UBN Tower.
Tel: 238-7057

British Airways
Wisma Merlin
Tel: 242-6177
Airport: 746-4417, 746-2600

Cathay Pacific Airways
UBN Tower
Tel: 238-3377
Airport: 746-1667

China Airlines
Bangunan Amoda, 22 Jalan Imbi
Tel: 248-9584, 242-7469
Airport: 746-5885, 746-3948

Czechoslovak Airlines
12th floor, Plaza Atrium,
10 Lorong P. Ramlee
Tel: 238-0176

Garuda Indonesian Airways
Bangunan Angkasa Raya,
123 Jalan Ampang
Tel: 242-0481, 248-4072
Airport: 746-2627

Japan Air Lines
Bangunan Pernas International,
Jalan Sultan Ismail
Tel: 261-1722
Airport: 746-5554

KLM Royal Dutch Airlines
Regent of Kuala Lumpur, Jalan

Sultan Ismail
Tel: 242-7011

Korean Airlines
17th floor, MUI Plaza, Jalan P.
Ramlee
Tel: 242-8311
Airport: 746-4745

Lufthansa
3rd floor, Bangunan Pernas
International, Jalan Sultan Ismail.
Tel: 261-4666.
Airport: 746-4433, 746-4441.

Malaysia Airlines
33rd floor, Bangunan MAS, Jalan
Sultan Ismail.
Tel: 261-0555, 746-3000
Airport: 746-4555

Northwest Orient Airlines
UBN Tower
Tel: 238-4355

Qantas Airways
UBN Tower, 10 Jalan P. Ramlee
Tel: 238-9133, 232-6544
Airport: 746-2557

Royal Brunei Airlines
1st floor, Wisma Merlin,
Jalan Sultan Ismail
Tel: 242-6155

Royal Jordanian
8th floor, MUI Plaza,
Jalan P. Ramlee
Tel: 248-7500
Airport: 746-3635

SAS (Scandinavian Airline System)
Bangunan Angkasa Raya
Tel: 242-6044

Sabena Belgian World Airlines
Wisma Stephens, Jalan Raja Chulan

Tel: 242-5244
Airport: 746-3250

Saudi Arabian Airlines
Bangunan Safuan,
7 Jalan Raja Abdullah
Tel: 298-4566, 298-4150
Airport: 746-3150

Singapore Airlines
2 Jalan Dang Wangi
Tel: 292-3122, 298-7033.
Airport: 746-3824.

Thai Airways International
Kuwasa Building, Jalan Raja Laut
Tel: 293-7100
Airport: 746-4999

Turkish Airlines
Hotel Equatorial, Jalan Sultan Ismail.
Tel: 261-4055

UTA French Airlines
7th floor, Plaza See Hoy Chan,
Jalan Raja Chulan
Tel: 232-6952

United Airlines
2nd floor, Bangunan MAS,
Jalan Sultan Ismail.
Tel: 261-1433

Yugoslav Airlines
4th floor, Menara Boustead,
69 Jalan Raja Chulan
Tel: 241-9245, 241-9454

Diplomatic Missions

All embassies are open Monday through Friday unless otherwise noted.

Argentine Embassy
3 Jalan Semantan 2,
Damansara Heights

Tel: 255-0176
Hours: 8 a.m. - 2 p.m.

Australian High Commission
6 Jalan Yap Kwan Seng
Tel: 242-3122/242-3462
Hours: 8.30 a.m. - 12 noon; 1.30 p.m. - 4 p.m.

Austrian Embassy
7th Floor, MUI Plaza,
Jalan P. Ramlee
Tel: 248-4277.
Hours: 8 a.m. - 4 p.m. Consular hours: 8 a.m. - 12 noon

Bangladesh High Commission
204-1 Jalan Ampang
Tel: 242-3271
Hours: 9 a.m. - 5 p.m.

Belgium Embassy
12 Lorong Yap Kwan Seng
Tel: 248-5733
Hours: 8 a.m. - 2 p.m

Brazilian Embassy
22 Pesiaran Damansara Endah
Tel: 254-8020
Hours: 8 a.m.- 2 p.m.

British High Commission
185 Jalan Ampang
Tel: 248-7122
Hours: 9 a.m. - 3.30 p.m.

Burmese Embassy
5 Taman U Thant Satu
Tel: 242-4085
Hours: 9 a.m. - 1 p.m., 2 p.m. - 5 p.m. Consular hours: 9 a.m. - 1 p.m.

Canadian High Commission
7th Floor, MBf Plaza,
Jalan Ampang
Tel: 261-2000
Hours: 8 a.m. - 4 p.m. Consular hours: 8 a.m. - 12.30 p.m.

Chinese Embassy
229 Jalan Ampang
Tel: 242-8495
Hours: 9 a.m. - 12 noon, 2.30 p.m.
- 5 p.m. Consular hours: 9 a.m. - 12
noon

Czechoslovakian Embassy
32 Jalan Mesra
Tel: 242-7185
Hours: 8.30 a.m. - 1.45 p.m., 2 p.m.
- 4 p.m.

Danish Embassy
22nd Floor, Bangunan Angkasa
Raya, Jalan Ampang
Hours: 9 a.m. - 4 p.m.

Egyptian Embassy
38 Lingkongan U Thant
Tel: 456-8184
Hours: 9 a.m. - 3 p.m. Consular
hours: 10 a.m. - 2 p.m.

Embassy of Finland
15th Floor, MBf Plaza,
Jalan Ampang
Tel: 2611088
Hours: 8.30 a.m. - 4.15 p.m.

Embassy of France
196 Jalan Ampang
Tel: 248-4122
Hours: 8 a.m. - 4 p.m. Consular
hours: 8.30 a.m. - 12.30 p.m.

Embassy of the German Democratic Republic
3 Jalan U Thant
Tel: 456-2894
Hours: 9 a.m. - 4 p.m. Consular
hours: 9 a.m. - 12 noon

Consulate of Iceland
74 Jalan Universiti, Petaling Jaya
Tel: 757-3745
Hours: 9 a.m. - 5 p.m.

Indian High Commission
20th Floor, Wisma Selangor
Dredging, Jalan Ampang
Tel: 261-7000
Hours: 9 a.m. - 1 p.m., 2 p.m. - 5.30
p.m. Consular hours: 9.30 a.m. -
12.30 p.m.

Indonesian Embassy
233 Jalan Tun Razak
Tel: 984-2011
Hours: 8 a.m. - 1 p.m., 2 p.m. - 4
p.m. Consular hours: 8:30 a.m. - 12
noon, 2 p.m. - 3 p.m.

Iranian Embassy
5 Jalan Mayang
Tel: 243-3575
Hours: 8.30 a.m. - 1 p.m., 2 p.m. -
4.30 p.m. Friday: 8.30 a.m. - 12.30
p.m.. Saturday: 8.30 a.m. - 3.30
p.m.

Iraqi Embassy
2 Jalan Langgak Golf,
off Jalan Tun Razak
Tel: 248-0555
Hours: 9 a.m. - 2 p.m.

Embassy of Ireland
2nd Floor, Straits Trading
Building, 4 Lebuh Pasar Besar
Tel: 298-5111
Hours: 8.30 a.m. - 1 p.m., 2 p.m. -
5 p.m. Saturday 8.30 a.m. - 1 p.m.

Italian Embassy
99 Jalan U Thant
Tel: 456-5122
Hours: 9 a.m. - 2 p.m. Consular
hours: 9 a.m. - 1.30 p.m.

Japanese Embassy
11 Jalan Tun Razak
Tel: 243-8044
Hours: 8.30 a.m. - 12.30 p.m., 2
p.m. - 4.30 p.m. Consular hours: 8
a.m. - 3.30 p.m.

Kuwaiti Embassy
229 Jalan Tun Razak
Tel: 948-6033
Hours: 9 a.m. - 1 p.m., 2 p.m. - 5 p.m.

Netherlands Embassy
4 Jalan Mesra
Tel: 243-1143
Hours: 9 a.m. - 3 p.m. Consular hours: 9 a.m. - 1 p.m.

New Zealand High Commission
193 Jalan Tun Razak
Tel: 248-6422
Hours: 8 a.m. - 12.30 p.m., 1.30 p.m. - 4.30 p.m. Consular hours: 10.30 a.m. - 12.30 p.m., 1.30 p.m. - 4.30 p.m.

North Korean Embassy
11A Jalan Delima
Tel: 984-7110
Hours: 8 a.m. - 5 p.m.

Norwegian Embassy
11th Floor, Bangunan Angkasa Raya, Jalan Ampang
Tel: 243-0144
Hours: 9 a.m. - 3 p.m.

Pakistan High Commission
132 Jalan Ampang
Tel: 241-8877
Hours: 9 a.m. - 1 p.m., 2 p.m. - 5 p.m. Friday: 9 a.m. - 12 noon

Philippine Embassy
1 Cangkat Kia Peng
Tel: 248-4233
Hours: 8.30 a.m. - 12 noon, 2 p.m. - 4 p.m.

Polish Embassy
495, 41/2 mile Jalan Ampang
Tel: 457-6733.
Hours: 8.30 a.m. - 12.30 p.m., 1.30 p.m. - 4 p.m.

Consular hours: 8.30 a.m. - 12.30 p.m.

Romanian Embassy
114 Jalan Damai, off Jalan Ampang
Tel: 248-2065
Hours: 8 a.m. - 2 p.m.

Saudi Arabian Embassy
7 Jalan Kedondong, off Jalan Ampang Hilir
Tel: 457-9433
Hours: 9 a.m. - 1 p.m., 2 p.m. - 3 p.m.

Singapore High Commission
209 Jalan Tun Razak
Tel: 261-6277
Hours: 8.30 a.m. - 1 p.m., 2 p.m. - 5 p.m.

South Korean Embassy
422 Jalan Tun Razak
Tel: 948-2177
Hours: 8.30 a.m. - 12.30 p.m., 2 p.m. - 4 p.m.

Soviet Embassy
263 Jalan Ampang
Tel. 456-7252
Hours: 8 a.m. - 3 p.m. Consular hours: 8 a.m. - 1 p.m.

Embassy of Spain
200 Jalan Ampang
Tel: 248-4868
Hours: 9 a.m. - 1 p.m., 2 p.m. - 5 p.m. Consular hours: 9 a.m. - 1:30 p.m.

Sri Lanka High Commission
18 Lorong Yap Kwan Seng
Tel: 242-3154
Hours: 8.30 a.m. - 1 p.m., 2 p.m. - 4.15 p.m.

Embassy of the Sultanate of Oman
24 Lingkongan U Thant,

off Jalan U Thant
Tel: 457-5011
Hours: 9 a.m. - 1 p.m., 2 p.m. - 4
p.m. Consular hours: 9 a.m. - 3 p.m.

Swedish Embassy
6th Floor, Bangunan Angkasa Raya,
Jalan Ampang
Tel: 248-5981
Hours: 8.30 a.m. - 3 p.m.

Embassy of Switzerland
16 Pesiaran Madge,
off Jalan U Thant
Tel: 248-0622
Hours: 8 a.m. - 5.30 p.m. Monday,
8 a.m. - 4.45 p.m. Tuesday and
Thursday, 8 a.m. - 1 p.m. Wednesday and Friday. Consular hours: 9
a.m. - 1 p.m.

Thai Embassy
206 Jalan Ampang
Tel: 248-8222
Hours: 9 a.m. - 1 p.m.,
2.30 a.m. - 5 p.m. Consular hours:
9 a.m. - 1 p.m.

Embassy of the United States of America
376 Jalan Tun Razak
Tel: 248-9011
Hours: 7.45 a.m. - 1 p.m., 2 p.m. -
4.30 p.m. Consular hours: 8.45 -
11.30 a.m.

Vietnamese Embassy
4 Pesiaran Stoner
Tel: 248-4036.
Hours: 8.30 a.m. - 12.30 p.m.,
2 p.m. - 4.30 p.m.
Saturday: 8.30 a.m. - 12 noon.

FURTHER READING

Malaysians are not avid readers, and this is reflected in the mediocre range of titles available at local bookstores, with perhaps the exception of the University of Malaya's bookshop. The larger stores devote a section to local interest, or Malaysiana, as the Berita Book Centre in Bukit Bintang Plaza calls it. Other bookstores include Times Distributors with branches in Sungai Wang Plaza and Weld Supermarket, Anthonian with outlets in Bangsar and Wilayah Complex, and MPH in Jaya Supermarket, Petaling Jaya. The titles here are only a selection of the publications available in Malaysia.

History

J.M. Gullick: *Kuala Lumpur 1880-1895*. Pelanduk Publications, Malaysia, 1988 edition. A detailed record of the birth and growth of Kuala Lumpur and its pioneers.

J.M. Gullick: *The Story of Kuala Lumpur (1857-1939)*. Eastern University Press, Malaysia, 1983. Well-written vivid account by the former Malayan civil service member.

Barbara Watson Andaya and Leonard Y Andaya: *A History of Malaysia*. Macmillan Editions Ltd, London, 1982

People, Culture and Arts

Kit Lee: *Adoi.* Times Books International, Singapore/Kuala Lumpur, 1989. A humorous, well-illustrated satire of Malaysian faces, foibles and fancies.

Tan Chee Beng: *The Baba of Melaka.* Pelanduk Publications, Kuala Lumpur 1988. An insight into a segment of Malaysia's society, the Chinese Peranakan, their identity, culture and customs.

Virginia H Danaz: *Women and Party Politics in Peninsula Malaysia.* Oxford University Press. A look at the nature of women's participation in the political process of multi-racial Malaysia.

ART/PHOTO CREDITS

Photography	**Ingo Jezierski**
Maps	**Berndtson & Berndtson**
Cover Design	**Klaus Geisler**

Index

112

W,Y,Z

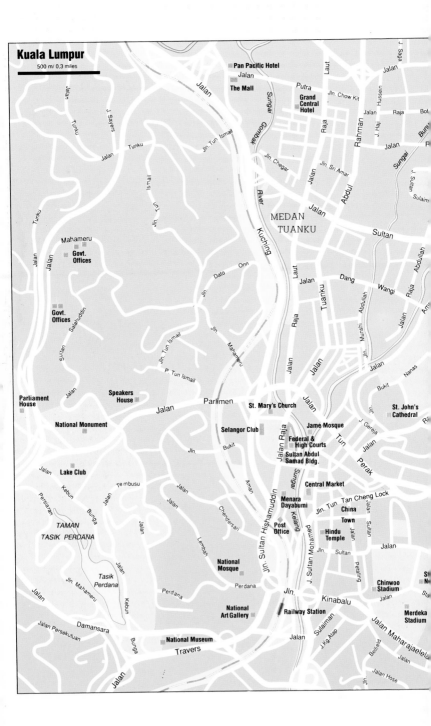

Kuala Lumpur

500 m/ 0.3 miles

Pan Pacific Hotel

The Mall

Putra

Grand Central Hotel

Jln. Chow Kit

MEDAN TUANKU

Jalan

Jalan Tunku

J. Sayers

Tunku

Jln. Tun Ismail

Jln. Chegar

Jln. Sri Amar

Raja

Rahman

J. Haji Hussein

Sungai

Raja

Bot

Jalan

Abdul

Sungai

Sultan

Sulaim

Jalan

Sultan

Ismail

Jln. Tun

Mahameru

Govt. Offices

Jln Dato Onn

Laut

Jalan

Dang Wangi

Raja Abdullah

Raja

Govt. Offices

Salahuddin

Jln. Tun Ismail

P. Tun Ismail

Jln. Mahameru

Raja

Tuanku

Jalan

Munshi

Abdullah

Jalan

Nanas

Sultan

Jalan

Bukit

Parliament House

Speakers House

Jalan Parlimen

St. Mary's Church

Jalan

Jln. J. Gereja

St. John's Cathedral

National Monument

Selangor Club

Jame Mosque

Jalan Raja

Federal & High Courts

Sultan Abdul Samad Bldg.

Jln.

Bukit

Aman

Tun

Perak

Jalan

Lake Club

Tembusu

Jalan

Jalan

Chenderasari

Lembah

Jalan Sultan Hishamuddin

Sungai

Klang

Central Market

Menara Dayabumi

Jln. Tun Tan Cheng Lock

China Town

Sultan

Kebun

Bunga

Jln. Mahameru

Kebun

Post Office

Hindu Temple

Jln. Sultan

Jalan

TAMAN TASIK PERDANA

Tasik Perdana

Jalan

Perdana

National Mosque

Perdana

J. Sultan Mohamed

Kinabalu

Petaling

Chinwoo Stadium

S. N

Sta

Jalan

Persiaran

Jalan Persekutuan

Damansara

Bunga

National Art Gallery

Railway Station

Sulaiman

Jln.

Merdeka Stadium

Jalan Maharajalela

National Museum

Travers

Jalan

J. Kg Atap

Jalan Hose

Jalan

Belfield

Jalan

Jln.

J. Saga

Jalan

Laut

Jalan

Bumi

Fi